About the Book

This book details the life of triathlete Brad Kearns, from his beginnings in the sport of triathlon, to life on the professional circuit, competing all over the globe against other top triathletes of the world.

Kearns offers a unique inside look at the challenges and rewards of succeeding in this relatively young but fast-growing sport—where many professional competitors struggle to make ends meet while dedicating their lives to the arduous training regimen and disciplined lifestyle required for success.

This self-effacing account of Kearns's athletic journey is laced with hilarious tales of mischief and high-risk adventure, in a sport where the unique, close-knit fraternity of athletes are cutthroat in competition, yet "cut-loose" off the race course.

What Others Say

This book is a refreshing departure from the common "how to" books in sports. Brad goes beyond the race results and workout miles to provide an intimate look at the lifestyle of a professional athlete. I highly recommend this book from one of the most colorful personalities in sports today.

Mark Allen
Triathlete of the decade

Besides his talent as an athlete, Brad Kearns is a helluva story teller. If you like endurance sports, you'll love this book.

Bob Babbitt
Publisher, Competitor Magazine

He does a wonderful job of depicting the sometimes exotic and sometimes neurotic lifestyle of a professional endurance athlete. He shares many of his memories, sometimes hilarious and sometimes deeply revealing, always interesting. I'd have read this book even if I didn't know a thing about triathlons.

Scott Tinley
Two-time Hawaii Ironman
Triathlon Champion

Can You Make a Living Doing That?

the true-life adventures of a professional triathlete

Brad Kearns

Published by The Trimarket Company, Palo Alto, California, USA

Library of Congress Cataloging-in-Publication Data

Kearns, Brad, 1965-
    Can you make a living doing that? : the true-life adventures of a professional tri-
athlete / Brad Kearns.
          p.   cm.
    ISBN 0-9634568-8-1 (alk. paper)
    1. Kearns, Brad, 1965-   2. Athletes—United States—Biography.
3. Triathlon. I. Title.
GV697. A1K34   1996
796'. 092—dc20   95-34990
                                                        CIP

Published by: The Trimarket Company, P. O. Box 60871, Palo Alto, California 94306

Photos: Tony Svensson. A special thanks to Kay King, and to Mike von Huene at United
Airlines SFOOT and Vince Bevilaqua at United Airlines SFOOR.
Cover design: Trimarket and Pixelmedia
Color separations: Pixelmedia
Text editing: Shannon Folena

Production notes: This book was created using FrameMaker® from Frame Technology
Corporation on PowerBook® and Power Macintosh® computers from Apple Computer,
Inc. The artwork was produced using Adobe Illustrator® and the photos managed with
Adobe Photoshop® from Adobe Systems, Inc.

Printed and bound in the United States of America

ISBN 0-9634568-8-1
Library of Congress Catalog Card Number: 95-34990

To Tracy, my best friend.

Only those who dare, truly live.

John Benun

CONTENTS

FOREWORD

"Can you make a *living* doing that?" is the first question most people ask me when I tell them I'm a pro triathlete. It's usually followed by "What will you do when you're through racing?" and "Is your wife a triathlete, too?" My standard retorts to these three questions are: "Sometimes," "What will *you* do when you're through with your job?" and finally, "Is your wife/husband a firefighter/accountant/video store clerk/ etc., too?"

I know that questions like these stem from the fact that most people have not spoken to very many pro triathletes. I'm not trying to be a wise guy with my retorts. I'm just trying to offer the perspective that it's just another job, albeit a most unusual one.

Unless you spend a lot of time on airplanes, getting to know a pro triathlete is difficult, as there aren't that many around. But, most everyone I have met during my career seem really interested in the life of a pro triathlete. So, I have created in this book an opportunity to read all about the life of one, and all the excitement, embarrassment, glory, struggles and adventure that I have experienced in my career.

I hope you enjoy the reading and look forward to the next time you meet a pro triathlete—in an airport terminal or on the trail. After reading this book, you will be able to wow them with your intelligent conversation and background knowledge about a sport and a lifestyle that is truly unique.

PROLOGUE—CAN'T SLEEP AGAIN

May 1993, Atlanta, Georgia, Stone Mountain Inn, the night before the DCA Atlanta Sprint Triathlon:

Race is tomorrow; I'm really looking forward to it. It's a "sprint" distance race, shorter than the usual races we compete in on the professional triathlon circuit, and I think the shorter distance will favor me. I felt great last weekend, winning a low-key sprint distance race in Sacramento. It was a great tune up and got my confidence high for the real thing tomorrow. The DCA Atlanta Sprint is the richest sprint race in the history of the sport with a $50,000 purse, including $7,000 for the winner. *God, seven grand! I'd love to go home with that check tomorrow... Don't even think about it, it's a hex! Much easier to think about winning than to actually do it.*

I can't sleep again, no big deal. I'm used to it the night before a race. My body's so wired, anxious and alert, I often just lie there with thoughts racing through my head. Most of them aren't about the race, just about life, but my mind is so active that falling asleep takes forever. Then I start thinking about the fact that I'm not falling asleep, which makes it even worse. At this point, what I usually do is pretend I'm asleep. I lie in bed, deeply relaxed, body "asleep" but the mind is still awake. It's a state where if someone said, "Hey Brad, you awake?" I'd answer immediately, "Yeah, whaddya want?"

I get up and go into the bathroom so I won't disturb my hotel roommate, a first year pro I just met named Nate Llerandi. I sit in the bathroom and start writing—what else to do? Pretty soon I have a decent training article going, about the benefits of training with my dog, Duane, which I'll send to *Triathlete* magazine for future publication. I write for about 45 minutes and then return to bed. My mind is a bit clearer, and I'm happy that at least I was able to be productive with my insomnia. *Maybe I'll even fall asleep.*

Rrrring! The wake up call comes at 5:30 AM Eastern time for the 7 AM race start. If I wanted to stress, I could shudder at the thought that I was waking up at 2:30 AM California time—but hey, I don't even think I fell asleep. I guess I could also stress about not sleeping; but I remember some of my worst races coming after sleeping soundly the night before. After those dismal efforts, I felt like I shouldn't have been that tired to sleep so well, that I was lacking the excitement and restless energy flowing through my body that hinders sleep but prepares you for a maximum race effort.

The worst moment in triathlon, for me, is wake up time on race morning. In addition to the typical ungodly hour, my first thoughts are usually anxiety about the moment finally arriving. I haven't felt really nervous about races since high school track, but if there is any time I still feel some of that sickening nervousness, it's then. I think about how much money is on the line in the race—and sometimes about how desperately I need it—and about how much I've sacrificed in my life to prepare for the moment of truth, soon to arrive.

Once in a while I panic and think that I don't even want to get up and race, that I'm not cut out for it, that I should just get a real job and not have to deal with this stress. I immediately counter these panic flashes with positive self-talk, such as: "I love being a triathlete," or "This race is the test; it's what you've trained so hard for, so just go out and do your best and be happy with that," or maybe just "Shut up—this is your job! Time to go to work." I always ponder my biggest fear— whether my body is ready to turn in a peak performance on that particular day. You would think I might know this after so many years of racing, but I never really find out until the race is underway whether I have the juice or not.

Everything gets better once I get out of bed and get moving. I immediately busy myself with the pre-race routine so my mind gets occupied with something other than negative, fearful thoughts. I usually allow less time than I need for pre-race preparations, so I can "sleep" as long as possible and then rush through my preparations right up until the gun goes off.

Experts always say allow plenty of time before the race, so you can calmly go about your preparations and deal with any unforeseen problems. But, I like having that hectic little edge of feeling rushed for time on race morning. It gets me pumped up for the race. Remember, don't try this at home!

Even though this Atlanta race is a big one, and I didn't get any sleep, I feel unusually calm when I wake up. Yesterday at the pre-race meeting for professionals, I looked around the room at my competition. Many top athletes were gathered in the room, but this strange feeling came over me as I looked around, a feeling that I was going to win the race. It was much more powerful than a verbal statement to the same effect, because an affirmative statement like, "I think I can win" is always somewhat forced. You can talk yourself into anything if you try hard enough, especially if people egg you on (e.g. "Hey Brad, you're a fast runner, you have a shot to win here, don't you think?")

The feeling returns when I wake up race morning, which is strange because I never dwell on how I might fare against other athletes. It's too damaging to get my hopes up and then be disappointed, or put extra pressure on myself if I happen to be a favorite. Instead, I always dwell and obsess on how I will fare regardless of my competition. I wonder about things like, "Am I ready to turn in a performance indicative of my fitness level? Am I overtrained and due to bomb out? Did I train enough in each event to be competitive? Is my swim still lacking? Will my knee hurt on the run?"

Race morning in Atlanta is different. My mind keeps drifting from my usual preoccupations to thoughts of winning the race. Maybe these thoughts are normal for someone who is used to winning every race, but it feels funny to me. *Just go with it; it's got to be a good sign.*

Up and out of bed. Wolf down some energy bars and my powdered drink, my calories for the race. I allow 15 minutes to get out of the room, get dressed in jacket and tights, fill up Bikestream water bottle (pressurized drinking system), pump up tires. Done. *I'm outta here.*

Before the race, I ride my bike for 20 minutes as warm-up.

The hotel is conveniently about that far away, so I arrive at the race site with my warm-up done. Then I set up my transition area where I park the bike and lay out my running shoes and racing singlet. To get into the transition area, which is restricted to athletes, we have to line up at the entrance and each get our race number marked on our bodies by volunteers with thick marking pens. I hate this part—they have to mark both arms, thighs and one calf, which means I have to pretty much strip down on this chilly morning, so they can gain access to all of my limbs. I don't like anyone touching me before a race—my body feels like it's on fire because I'm so wired and I just want to keep all that energy for myself. It's worsened when the volunteer marking me is a female, and she makes a suggestive comment as an attempt at humor—something about me stripping in front of her, or her feeling my muscles, shaved legs, whatever. In this situation, I usually smile politely and think, "Don't you get tired of making the same silly comments to everyone you mark?" Well, maybe not. *There has to be some reason why you volunteer to get up at 5 AM to pen numbers on people's bodies!*

After the bike ride, body marking and transition setup, I go jog for a few minutes and hopefully take care of some last minute business with my plumbing. There are always a few port-a-potties at races, but in the morning the lines are horrendous. I look at everyone standing in line and wonder if they allotted time in their morning schedules to stand in the bathroom line for 15 minutes. No chance for me and my hectic schedule—I always bring a roll of toilet paper from the hotel and find a nice quiet place along my jogging route.

I return from my jog to the transition area, running late as usual. Most of the pros are zipping their wetsuits and walking down to the swim start at the beach.

OK, take off sweats and stuff them in backpack. Remember to coat thighs and neck with vaseline, so the wetsuit rubber won't chafe. Oh God, I'm the last one left in the transition area, guess everyone's at the beach. Better hurry and put the wetsuit on. Whoops, almost tripped. Oh yeah, I forgot, you can't "hurry" and put a wetsuit on. OK, it's on. Jog down to beach. Cool; looks like they're not organized yet and we won't start right on time. Now I can go out and warm-up. Ooooh, water's cold! Thank God for the wetsuit. What did we do before wet-

suits? Oh yeah, we froze!

I finish the warm-up, feeling great and return to the starting line. We stand in the chilly water of Stone Mountain Lake forever as the race start is delayed with traffic problems on the bike course. Finally, with everybody freezing and shivering from the long wait, the gun goes off for a frenzied 800 meter swim. Normally we swim 1,500 meters in the Olympic distance races [1,500 meter swim (.9 mile), 40 kilometer bike (24.8 miles) and 10 km run (6.2 miles)] that are most common on the triathlon circuit. Since swimming is my weakest even, the shortened swim is great for me.

Before I know it, we hit the beach. *Wow, done already! That was fast, I wonder how I'm doing? There's my friend Scott in the crowd,* "Go Brad, you're only 15 seconds behind the leader!" *Yeahhhh!!! That's great for me.* I'm usually further back, but now I can see everyone in front of me as we run from the lake to the parking lot to mount our bikes. *OK, reached the bike. My feet are frozen. God, that barefoot run hurt! Gotta get out of this full length, skin-tight, neoprene wetsuit as fast as possible and get going. Tug, pull, ahhhh! It's off! I'm doing great! No one's even riding yet, they're all here. Put on sunglasses, buckle helmet. GO!*

I take my bike off the rack and mount it barefoot with my shoes already affixed to the pedals. The fastest way to start is to get the heck on the bike and start pedaling with your bare feet smashing down your shoes on the pedals. Then when you attain a decent speed, reach down and slip one foot into the shoe and velcro it closed, then pedal for a bit to return to speed, reach down and secure the other foot in the shoe.

Oh yes, my transition was awesome! I'm the fourth guy out of the bike racks, made up all 15 seconds. Come on legs, lets go! OK, got some speed, left foot in, velcroed. Right foot. Whoaaa!

I hit a giant speed bump with only one hand on the bars, the other on my shoe. My front wheel twists sideways in the air like a moto-cross rider. I land and the bike shoots sideways.

Holy cow! I'm lucky to be upright. Glad I didn't hit anyone else. Phew, took my breath away. OK, settle down, right foot in, velcroed. I guess that was the speed bump they were talking about in the pre-race meeting yesterday!

I'm still freezing from that stupid 30-minute wait and the cold water swim. I can't feel my feet at all, and my hands aren't too warm either. *Come on, warm up, breathe, start sweating. Hey, where is everybody? I'm in the lead! I'm freezing and I'm in the lead! Look back, anyone come with me up here? No! Wonder where Jimmy* (Riccitello—a strong cyclist) *is? He always comes through the field on the bike. Maybe it is my day today.*

My legs feel great! I never get the lead this early. I could get used to this! Nothing beats the sound of police sirens, loud police sirens, because you're close to them, clearing traffic ahead and announcing the arrival of the front of the race.

I can't believe this! Where is everybody? I was just trying to get warm. Forget them, lets just sneak off and dump them for good before they wake up and form a pack or something and work together to catch me. Let them play around however they want in the race for second!

Here comes that big hill, lets see how the legs really feel. You can often fool yourself on the flats, like those training rides where you just fly, going one direction, feeling awesome, only to turn around and face a huge, miserable headwind going back home. *Wow! I feel powerful. Keep pumping, stay in the big chainring. Hey, aren't there some primes on the course somewhere?* A prime ("preem") is a cash bonus given to whoever first reaches certain pre-designated points on the course. *Damn, I didn't pay attention when they described where the prime banners are because I never lead early in races. Hey, what's that banner? A prime! Ka-ching, 350 bucks, thank you.*

Anybody behind? Wow, out of sight! Now, I'm even more psyched. Keep pumping, time to put this one away early and for good. Keep pumping, more hills, take the pain, it's worth it, you can jog the run if you just take all the pain now. Take it now! Come on, it's only 12 miles, we've gotta be done soon. Forget about me guys!

Here's the transition area. "25 second lead Brad." *All right, that's all I need, it's only a 3-mile run, and I'm floating today. No one's gonna catch me—don't even look back. Just run the first mile hard, then relax. OK, there's the mile mark, now just run the second mile hard, then you can relax. OK, there's the 2-mile mark. Hey, another prime banner. Ka-ching! $350. Just run the third mile hard, then you can relax.*

What a weird place to put the banner, we're almost done with the race. Like what are the chances someone other than the winner will pick up the last prime? What a top heavy race, I'm gonna win $7,700. Wow! Now I look kind of funny calling and writing the race director beforehand to complain that the purse is top heavy.

Come on idiot, don't daydream! Concentrate on the race, you're almost done, one more mile, just enjoy it. OK, forget that. Hard to enjoy pain, and I'm definitely feeling the day's effort now. Concentrate and let's get it over with. We finish at the foot of Stone Mountain. There's the carvings, pretty cool... and there's the finish, even more cool!

Ahhhh, winning's more fun than anything! Why can't I do this—feel this good—every time out? I wish I knew, I'd bottle it up and sell it.

I won't soon forget this one.

1

THE ORIGIN OF THE PRO TRIATHLETE

The origin of the sport of triathlon is in dispute, but early multisport endurance events began appearing in San Diego in the late 1970s, so many like to stake claim that it originated there. When professional competition started appearing in the early 1980s, the center of that universe was definitely San Diego, specifically the north county coastal communities like La Jolla, Del Mar, Solana Beach, Cardiff, Encinitas and Carlsbad. The area was headquarters for the notorious Team JDavid, a fully sponsored, lavishly supported team of triathletes that included practically all of the world's best, including Mark Allen, Scott Molina and Scott Tinley. Unfortunately, the benefactor of these triathletes' tremendous support, Jerry Dominelli, headed the investment firm JDavid, which turned out to be a large fraudulent investment scheme. In all, some $200 million was taken in, $50 million of which was squandered on the extravagant life-styles of the principals and their far-reaching philanthropy in the San Diego sporting, arts and education circles. JDavid was the darling of the community until the pyramid scheme came crashing down in 1984. Many investors lost all or most of their money, the triathletes lost their sponsorship, and Dominelli got a prison sentence.

Before their dream situation collapsed, JDavid athletes were largely responsible for creating a life-style, that of a true "professional" triathlete, supported by sponsorship and prize money, training all day in pursuit of excellence in their growing sport.

Since the best athletes were training in the ideal weather of San Diego, most everyone who was serious about challenging them relo-

1

cated to the area, creating a snowball effect on the triathlon population in San Diego—and in Boulder, Colorado during the summer. Athletes from all over the world still flock to these training headquarters. Last year, Scott Tinley remarked that he needed a Berlitz dictionary to communicate with many of the participants on San Diego's infamous Tuesday morning run.

The Ironman, the crown jewel of the sport, began in 1978 on the island of Oahu, created—as the often told legend goes—by Navy Seal John Collins and a few of his comrades debating which was the toughest sporting event on the Hawaiian islands: the Waikiki Rough Water Swim of 2.4 miles, the Dick Evans Memorial Bike Race of 112 miles around the island of Oahu, or the 26.2-mile Honolulu Marathon. The small group decided to quell the argument by attempting to do all three in one day. That would surely be the toughest event in the islands! So, 14 hardy souls organized and participated in the first Ironman, won by Gordon Haller in 11 hours, 38 minutes. Word soon spread after a *Sports Illustrated* feature article on 1979 winner Tom Warren and his outrageous exercise habits. When the curiosity of ABC's Wide World of Sports was piqued, the Hawaii Ironman began to enter the consciousness of endurance-minded athletes everywhere.

In 1980, a swim coach from Davis, California, named Dave Scott obliterated the field and the course record, finishing in 9 hours, 23 minutes. His incredible performance ushered in the era of the professional triathlete; Dave was the first who literally trained all day for triathlons and was able to make a living at it.

The size of the Ironman fields and the number of triathlons and triathletes nationwide mushroomed in the early 80s, buoyed by Julie Moss's collapse and crawl across the finish line at the February 1982 Ironman, which inspired millions of people watching ABC's telecast. Professional competitions began to appear as television became interested in duplicating the extremely popular Ironman program shown annually. The first ever Triathlon World Championship was held in Nice, France in 1982 and was won by a California lifeguard and member of Team JDavid named Mark Allen. He would go on to completely dominate that event—and the sport for that matter—winning all ten times he entered Nice. He would also win five consecutive Hawaii Ironmans and enjoy two undefeated seasons.

The Ironman is now a multimillion dollar property and a corporate entity. There are six official Ironman races contested worldwide; the premier event in Hawaii turns down thousands of applicants each year to limit its field to 1,500. The female record time of 8 hours, 55 minutes—by seven-time winner Paula Newby-Fraser of Zimbabwe (who resides in San Diego and Boulder)—is faster than many of the male winning times from the early years of the race.

Mark Allen continues to lower his own men's record. His 1993 time was 8 hours, 7 minutes. The lead bikers now average a phenomenal 25 miles per hour for the 112 miles, and Mark Allen and Dave Scott, in their epic duel in the 1989 race, both ran close to six-minute miles for the entire marathon. At the end of that long day, in the intense afternoon heat of the Kona Coast—after nearly 140 miles of racing—Mark Allen *sprinted away* from Dave Scott. What was once a survival contest is now a flat-out race. If you want to be competitive with the best as a pro or even in the hotly-contested age divisions, every minute counts, and you had better be prepared to race the entire day.

Beyond the Ironman, triathlon is today contested by more than two million people in over 100 countries worldwide on every continent. The sport has been accepted into the Olympics for the year 2000 in Sydney, Australia.

2

A QUARTERBACK OR A RUNNER?

My introduction to "triathlon training" dates back to early childhood, when I first learned to ride a bike. Growing up in Woodland Hills, a suburb of Los Angeles in the San Fernando Valley, I participated in various sports leagues during the school year. Summers were spent biking around the neighborhood, swimming in the pool with friends (the Valley is famous for having a pool in every backyard), and of course running around and just playing games in the street.

Sports were always the focal point of my life; I remember being mesmerized by television coverage of the 1972 Olympics in Munich, West Germany, when I was seven years old. I immediately began training for the Olympics in my backyard, setting up a high jump crossbar and a pit made with bean bags (it was the 1970s, a long jump runway and landing pit, and fashioning a javelin out of a bamboo stick, which doubled as the high jump bar. Every day after school in the second grade, I would head to the backyard and commence training in the different events.

I was always involved in sports leagues, including soccer, flag football, basketball, track & field, golf, and baseball. I wanted to succeed in sports more than anything, but I was small for my age and also a year younger than my classmates, so I was certainly not a star, particularly in Los Angeles where there is plenty of competition. Several kids in the neighborhood ended up in the college and professional levels in the major sports.

I had always dreamed of being a quarterback in the NFL, even faced with the reality that I was a little guy who was just a decent athlete. Relative to my peers, my talent lay not in athletics, but in academics. I scored highly on those tests they give to kids, and it was decided I would skip the first grade when I entered public school in 1971.

This became a source of frustration for me—it put me further behind physically, and thus athletically, and I didn't care to be a smart kid, just an athlete. I rebelled by goofing off in school, doing only what was required, rather than applying and challenging myself academically.

I was finally starting to give up on my pro football dream after playing a year of tackle football in seventh grade. Weighing in at 77 pounds in full pads in a 100-pound-and-under league, I sat on the bench every game and got slammed around in practice enough times to realize that football may not have been my calling.

Finally, in eighth grade, I found something I was best at— long distance running. It helped that I was at a small private school, Meadow Oaks, in Calabasas, with very little competition. We would have track meets against other private schools, and no one came near me in the mile, the longest event contested. I ran a best of 6:11 in eighth grade and 5:18 in ninth grade. I was finally assuming an identity from athletic success that I had long desired, that of the school's "runner." Actually, I had received that acclaim before as the kid who would always chase the ball whenever it got away. I was like Mikey from the famous Life cereal TV commercial, "Let Brad get it, he *likes* running after it."

My recognition as a runner had a positive effect on me. I wasn't good or big enough to be known as the all-around jock and certainly didn't want to be known as a brain, so I was happy being known as the runner. This was significant at Meadow Oaks, since the Director of the school, Vic Cook, was a super-jock himself and gave priority and recognition to athletic success. He was the best pole vaulter in the world for his age, jumping 14 feet 6 inches, a height competitive with a top high school vaulter, when he was 54 years old! Having a positive environment where one receives recognition for achievements from peers, parents and other role models, is beneficial for building confidence and acquiring motivation and discipline.

My parents, Gail and Walter, were always supportive of my younger siblings Jeff, Kathleen and me, not only in athletics, but in whatever endeavor we chose. They never put pressure on us. They simply let us explore all the options and encouraged us in whatever activities we chose.

They were a contrast to the typical success-oriented "little league" parents, who are prevalent in affluent areas like Woodland Hills. Often highly successful and motivated parents want the same for their children and will hover all over them to insure the same results.

I saw dozens of cases where kids were placed under extreme pressure by their parents to succeed at a young age. Typically this led to total rebellion by the time they reached high school. Luckily, I was able to laugh at the regularly occurring incidents during youth sports leagues where parents would make total fools of themselves berating their kid for a mistake or carrying on in the stands like the game was the world championship. What a way to grow up!

Although similar overbearing behavior occurred in academics, it was less apparent since it was usually confined to the home. I experienced one of the highest pressure academic environments imaginable entering junior high in the seventh grade. I attended Harvard School for boys in North Hollywood, a rigorous college prep school with a high snob factor attended mostly by rich kids from the Valley and Beverly Hills. In my case, it was a failed one-year experiment by my parents, who urged me to go there, thinking it was the best education available.

I was bribed by my well-meaning father to take the entrance exam for admission. I had no interest in doing it, but he said all I had to do was take the exam, and then he would buy me the new bowling ball I coveted. I decided to take him up on it, but I planned to purposefully flunk the test, so I wouldn't have to risk getting accepted and attend the school. My dad drove me to Harvard one Saturday to take the test. Once I got into the lecture hall with the hundreds of eager, nervous kids, the importance of it hit me, and I chickened out on throwing the result. I tried my best, and a few weeks later I received an acceptance letter to the school in the mail.

I put up a fuss about going. So, my dad upped his offer to a new bike if I would attend Harvard for a year and see how it went. I took a school tour and was awed by their tremendous facilities, including a modern, college-sized library, fully stocked laboratories for science classes, a TV and movie production studio, a full-sized gymnasium, tennis courts, a 100-yard football field and running track, all on a beautiful sprawling campus in Coldwater Canyon in North Hollywood. The seventh grade curriculum featured classes in four languages, on-camera work in the TV studio, a movie project, a field trip to Yosemite National Park, and various exchanges with their sister school, Westlake School for Girls in Holmby Hills.

The tour was given by a really cool recruiter named Mr. Michaud, who emphasized how fun all the PE facilities were and how often we would hook up with the Westlake girls. "Oh, you like sports? Cool! Yeah, we're gonna play football, basketball, soccer, tennis, track, everything. You like girls? Well, we have dances, parties, school visits, coed trips to Friday night football games, you name it!"

His buddy-to-buddy sales pitch about how I was so fortunate to have passed the test and be offered the chance to attend Harvard, along with the awe-inspiring campus tour suckered me in—I signed on the dotted line to attend seventh grade that coming fall.

Mr. Michaud turned out to be a pretty hard-ass social studies teacher, and he once said something that I have never forgotten. It actually helped to motivate me athletically for years afterwards. Our class was filled with a bunch of twelve and thirteen year old boys who had a lot on their mind besides social studies. We had many jock-types in the class as sports were heavily emphasized at Harvard and participation in them were weighed seriously in consideration for admission. Mr. Michaud coached the baseball team and liked to talk sports with the class on occasion. On a particularly unruly day, I guess we set him off enough for him to launch into a lecture on the importance of emphasizing education over sports. He delivered the old song and dance about how a career in athletics is fleeting and out-of-reach for most while education can prepare you for a successful life. He started his tirade with the following statement:

"Let me tell you all something. When I was young, I was a much better athlete than *any* of you will *ever* be! I played third base and was given a tryout with the California Angels! Well, it didn't work out because... (I forgot, something like he injured his shoulder), and I'm really glad I was serious about my education so I could fall back on something. So all you guys who think you're these big star jocks, well you better remember,..."

Since my dreams of being a pro quarterback were still foremost on my mind, his little lecture annoyed me greatly. How did he know what kind of athletes we were going to be when we got older? How could he say he was better? The memory would return to me frequently over the years and would always leave a bitter taste in my mouth, even though I understand it was a well-intentioned lecture to a bunch of kids. Perhaps if he had left out the first part about being better than any of us ever will, I would have taken his lecture more to heart.

The pressure at school was unbelievable, and it was a constant struggle to keep up. I felt it was a little early in my schooling to be driven with a proverbial whip. Although the educational opportunity was unsurpassed, I hated every minute of it. I couldn't imagine thriving there for six years.

I will never forget one incident which perfectly illustrated the overdose of pressure and parental influence present. One morning in my car pool to school, a classmate of mine was discussing the status of various homework assignments with his mom, who was driving. He suddenly became agitated when he realized that *she* had forgot to work with him on an assignment that was due shortly. I was amazed! I couldn't even imagine my parents being that overbearing about my homework, or anything else in my life.

This kid was on the fast track to becoming a doctor. I later found out he lasted something like two months as a first-year medical student, then dropped out to become an artist. Maybe he would have made a good doctor someday if left to his own devices, or perhaps he would have become an artist, anyway.

I was granted my walking papers from Harvard after seventh grade and enjoyed the next two years of junior high (in Los Angeles at the time junior high was three years, and high school was tenth, eleventh, and twelfth grades) at the smaller, low key environment at Meadow Oaks.

At Meadow Oaks, I began to pursue running further and started competing in ten kilometer (10K or 6.2 miles) road races on the weekends. On minimal training these affairs were quite painful—each race would knock me out for a couple of days afterwards. The length was just too much for my fitness level and training schedule. I soon burned out on the road racing scene, particularly when I discovered that there were many kids my age that were actually faster than me.

By the time I entered Taft High School in the fall of 1979, I had given up on running. I was looking forward to trying out for quarterback on the B football team (my seventh grade football experience long forgotten, I guess) and playing on the golf team in the spring. I went to register for football and saw the gymnastics coach, Ed Gunny, at the sign-up desk. I had met him the previous summer while running laps at the Taft track as he was an avid runner. He urged me to sign up for something I had never heard of—cross-country. He explained that it was long-distance running, and I told him no thanks. I was going to play football. He couldn't believe it!

I showed up for football practice the first day of school. They had already been through summer practice and the infamous hell week where they would hold brutal practices twice a day in the heat of late summer. They had told me at registration to go to the coach on the first day of school and ask him if I could sign up late for the football team. Surely they would love to have a 5 foot 5 inch, 115 pound quarterback with no experience lead the team to victory! The team came out to the field for practice dressed in full uniform. As they walked past me, I took one look at the size of the players (at first thinking the B team was the Varsity), turned around and walked home. The next day I joined the cross-country team.

The sophomore cross-country course was only two miles, and I figured I could handle that. When practice started, I realized I was still pretty burned out on running. I took to hiding in the bathroom, with my friend from elementary school Robert Benun, in a gas station just off campus as the team left for their workouts. After the group passed by on their run, we would leave the bathroom and sneak home early. When I won the first race of the season, with Robert following in second, many of our teammates didn't even know who we were! As the season progressed, and I started to attain decent results, I began to enjoy running a bit more.

3

A TACO TAKES ITS TOLL

I became a pretty serious runner during my three years at Taft High School. From my beginnings of hiding in the bathroom to avoid workouts, running became the focal point of my life. The success I achieved was a major source of self-esteem, which is often elusive during the teenage years. I wasn't very well-rounded as I was pretty shy socially, particularly at the huge Taft High, where there were over 800 students in each class. It was easy to get lost in the crowd in such an environment; any way I could distinguish myself was beneficial. Since my notoriety came in the rather obscure realm of long distance running, most of my social life and success in that area revolved around members of the cross-country and track teams.

Taft was a very apathetic school when it came to sports, and the distance runners were a small and largely unmotivated group. By the time we were seniors, a handful of serious Taft runners took to training with runners at El Camino Real, a neighboring high school. They had a large, close-knit team and regimented workouts. El Camino runners would regularly get together after meets for pizza feasts and weekend parties. These outings were fantastic; they offered camaraderie and some recognition for the running achievements that would be ignored at Taft, where popularity contests were the favored form of competition.

The El Camino Real team was led by Steve Dietch, an outstanding runner and my nemesis on the race course throughout high school. Steve would come out on top against me most of the time. He trained relentlessly and never broke down. I always strived to keep up with his workload, usually without success as I battled overtraining and injuries throughout high school. My results were inconsistent, but when I felt strong and healthy, I would be in the thick of things with the top area runners and was always capable of a big upset.

Training with Steve throughout high school, I never got complacent or suffered from a lack of competition. It tremendously helped my development. He would hammer me in training a couple days a week. Then we would race each other in high school meets throughout the cross-country and track seasons and at numerous weekend races.

By the time we were seniors, we were among the top runners in the nation at Junior Olympic meets, and among the top runners in the Los Angeles City high school district. We enjoyed reaching our main goals like breaking our respective school records on the cross-country course and getting invited to run in the high school division of the prestigious indoor Sunkist Invitational track meet—alongside the world's best track and field athletes—at the LA Sports Arena.

In the spring of my senior year, my goal was to make it to the state track and field championships, held in Sacramento that June. Steve had established himself as the best miler in the city early in the season and easily won the city championships. I was having a far more difficult time and I barely made the qualifying out of our little West Valley league, running a pedestrian 4:37 mile.

The night before the city semifinals meet, Steve and I joined some others to dine at the Red Onion Mexican restaurant. In the middle of the night I awoke with a stomach swollen to the size of a basketball and became violently ill. Of course the impenetrable Steve had no symptoms while the next day I felt like I would be serving up some more tacos any minute. I was nauseous and dizzy and barely made it from class to class before collapsing in my seat, dreading the time I would have to step onto a track across town and run in the biggest meet of the year. I remember driving a car pool of rowdy athletes to East Los Angeles College, struggling to keep focused and stay in my lane.

Somehow I made it to the starting line of my first event, the mile. I was certain that I would have to drop out, but I decided I should at least start the race. Once moving, my competitive juices flowed, along with the realization that this was my final high school race unless I qualified for city finals. I dug as deep as I ever had in my life and won the race, qualifying for finals the following week with my best time ever, 4 minutes, 24 seconds. After the race, I was sick in the infield for quite a while and staggered through the two-mile race later in the meet, finishing in last place. That was terribly disappointing since I was one of the favorites in the two-mile after upsetting all of the top runners in the city the previous week with a vicious kick on the last lap.

The newspaper article on the meet ran the headline "Taco takes toll in city semifinals," and discussed how Dietch had invited me to dine the previous night with his team at the restaurant where I got sick while he suffered no ill effects. All of us who ate at the Red Onion got quite a kick out of the article, and I felt fortunate that I had at least made it to finals in the mile.

I received another benefit—indeed a revelation—from the whole experience, one that occurred to me as I was on my hands and knees, puking my guts out. I had never felt more miserable physically, yet I had just run my best time ever for the mile. I was shocked that I was able to pull off such a performance. I realized that the mind is very powerful and can be used positively or negatively, for I had convinced myself all day that I would perform miserably. When the gun went off, I was able to ignore the negative thoughts and the physical illness and let my legs run fast, astonishing myself in the process. I felt like I had discovered this tremendous power in my body, an ability to summon a peak performance under the worst conditions imaginable. It wasn't some magical power as I was totally cooked for the two-mile later in the evening, and no mind power could change that. But the amount of suffering I was able to endure did wonders for my confidence and belief in myself as an athlete.

To qualify for State I needed to place in the top four in the mile at City Finals. I felt terrible as soon as the race started and the entire field dropped me after the first lap. I struggled around the track, watching my ultimate high school goal fade away with each passing lap. At the bell, with Dietch leading a tight pack, I was a full 50 yards behind the next to last place runner. At that point the disgust with my performance reached a breaking point and I just forgot about the pain and took off, at first determined to catch someone and not finish last. I was always known for my strong final lap kick, and the strength I felt in my body this time was unbelievable. I caught the next to last man on the backstretch, then swung wide on the homestretch, battling two other runners side by side for the final spot. One collapsed on the track five yards from the finish, and I out-leaned the other for fourth place.

I had made it to State! I finished in 4 minutes, 23 seconds, with my final lap time 59 seconds, my fastest finish ever. My dad filmed the whole race with a primitive home video camera, but he got so excited on the last lap that the camera was shaking the whole time, and all you could see on the film was me running way behind at the bell lap, and then suddenly appearing at the finish line battling with the others.

4:23 was pretty slow among the qualifiers from all over the state. When I arrived in Sacramento, I discovered from the meet entry form that my time was 24th out of the 27 State qualifiers. I laughed when I saw it, feeling no pressure, just wanting to run a fast time. There were two qualifying heats on Friday night, with the first five in each heat making it to the finals on Saturday night. My heat went out in a very slow pace, setting up a fast finish, perfect for me. I took off on the last lap and ran another 59, passing several runners, including Mr. City Champ Steve Dietch, and finished fifth in 4:19, qualifying for finals with my best time ever. My mother had flown up to watch the meet Friday night, and I was so certain of not qualifying for the finals that I told her to book her airline ticket to fly home Saturday. She had to change her reservation to stay and watch the finals race on Saturday night!

In the finals with the big boys, I discovered I was overmatched. The pace went out slow again, and at halfway I was right there with visions of another strong kick and a big upset. On the third lap, the leaders took off like a shot and left me hanging out by myself, and I finished my final high school race in last place. Well, maybe "9th in the State" sounds better! The experience of getting that far unexpectedly, even though I got pounded in the State final, was a tremendous confidence builder, and I ended my high school running career on what I felt was a high note.

My running career gave me great enjoyment, satisfaction and confidence in high school, mostly from the sense of accomplishment and the end results. I dreaded and despised the actual racing. Racing the mile on the track remains the most painful endeavor I have ever undertaken in my life.

As a runner, I was long on desire and guts and a little short on hard training. I was able to compete on a high level due to the former, but I paid the price by continually digging deep and giving every ounce of energy I had in the races. I liken it to being a great driver of a crummy race car. I could push the car to the limit and go really fast, but the car wasn't built (well enough trained) to go that fast, so it was very temperamental and frequently ended up in the shop for repairs.

Repeatedly going to the well and suffering monumentally did something to my brain, and I developed a tremendous anxiety towards racing. The more important the race, the more nervous and sick with fear I would become when race day approached. I would tell myself that I was being silly, that the race wasn't that important, so I didn't need to be so nervous. But whenever I got into a race, I cared deeply about every result, and I would always try my hardest. I would dutifully record every detail and split time of all my races, and cut out and save all relevant newspaper articles. If I ever gave less than my best, I would be terribly disappointed with myself.

My anxiety reached the point where I would feel exhausted and lethargic for the entire day of a track or cross-country meet. I would get to the meet and not even have the strength or desire to stretch or jog to warm up. I'd lie down in the stands and force myself to get up and jog right before my race started, my head filled with negative thoughts about how bad it was going to hurt or how tired and terrible I felt. Often I was unable to click into the race mode when the gun went off, and I would drift back from the leaders early in the race as I did in the mile at city finals. At some point in the race, my brain and body would react in desperation as I fell out of contention, and I would summon a fast and furious finish, ending the race totally spent.

Waiting around in mental anguish before each race, I would always ask myself, "What the hell am I doing this for?" The pre-race answer was never clear, usually something like, "Yeah, what am I doing here? Why don't I just go home?" Or, "I really don't care about this race, I'm just going to drop out." After each race, however, I always had a clear answer for why I participated, which I guess was why I always came back for more. The sense of accomplishment and recognition was a primary motivation; but something else, something inherent in the effort itself, was a powerful attraction for me.

To summon the will to push my body to the limit and experience the freedom and simplicity of running as fast as I could, without interference from the brain and self-doubting thoughts, was tremendously satisfying. At this point, the mind and body are in harmony, completely focused in the present and the physical act taking place. Many athletes have experienced this high state of consciousness as being in the "zone." Sometimes it feels like everything is in slow motion, or that there is no awareness of pain, or the crowd screaming in the background. Or it feels like the body is on autopilot—whether it's throwing pitch after pitch, making shot after shot, or running stride after stride—with no conscious effort or thought required. Whatever the activity, it is a very powerful and compelling sensation—addicting in a way.

Likewise, I'd feel a strange sensation when pushing myself to the edge to reach maximum effort. Time would freeze—I would no longer be focused on how far I'd run, how many laps to go, or what my pace was. It felt like I was running in a vacuum, completely unaware of the progression of time related to my effort, focused just on the effort itself. I'd also be unaware of anything extraneous, the crowd, the scenery along the course, people cheering for me or yelling out times. Instead I'd become aware of silly little things like that my feet were burning up on the hot track, or that I had slobber on my chin, or that the guy I was running behind had a stain on his uniform. Then after the race a friend would come up to me and say, "Did you hear your split time? I screamed it right in your face." And I'd be thinking, "Gosh, I didn't see you or hear anything, but that tag on my jersey really itched during the last mile."

Finishing the race and ending the pain was nothing short of euphoric, not simply because I could suddenly breathe but because of the body's well-known release of endorphins in the aftermath of a supreme effort. It seemed like all of my senses were hyperfunctioning for hours after a hard race—my legs and body felt like they were floating. I was more alert and witty after a race, everything was funnier, food tasted better, and I wouldn't even get tired. Of course I would get plenty tired later as the post-race endorphin high wore off.

This pattern of pre-race anxiety finally started to fade towards the end of high school as my confidence and fitness increased. When I began competing in triathlons, I enjoyed the competition much more, and the fact that the races lasted so much longer than running lessened their intensity and pressure. Triathlons can hurt; there is little comparable to the prolonged agony of an Ironman or racing a 10K full-bore with a body already fatigued from swimming and cycling, but to me that pain is more manageable.

Many people would have a much easier time handling the pain of a race of a few minutes than one lasting a few hours. But for me the memories of running track still cause me to feel nervous and queasy whenever I set foot on a track, even for a mere workout. When I do track workouts, I always warm up away from the track, running around the neighborhood or the campus. When I return, I try to get the workout over with as fast as possible, so I jump right into the hard stuff, and I have a very difficult time going anything less than full speed. It's the "wham, bam, lets get the hell out of here" track workout!

4

OFF TO COLLEGE?

Although I was thriving as a high school runner, I had neglected my academic career, and gaining acceptance into a good college was pretty dicey.

My main goal in the classroom had been to become the class clown, and I paid little attention to the teachers and their lessons. Once I spent a whole semester of ninth grade bringing stacks of old *Sports Illustrated* to class and cutting out pictures to make a giant collage. By the time the school year ended, it took up a whole wall in my room, about eight feet by six feet!

In high school I was notorious for reading the sports page, and eating, during class. I would read two sports sections, the *Daily News* and the *Los Angeles Times*, every day. By second period, I would start into parts of my infamous, well-stocked lunch bag, and be finished by lunchtime. Then I would walk home, frequently accompanied by a few friends, to feast on more from the vast selection in the Kearns' refrigerator. I would frequently get busted in class for eating, reading, talking with classmates, and generally not paying attention. My sophomore year I got marked down an entire grade in a photography class—from a B to a C—on the very last day of school, for reading the sports page after being disciplined several times throughout the semester.

This behavior was a source of frustration for my parents and teachers. The only thing that ever caused me to be concerned about grades was peer pressure and competition, particularly in high school when most of my friends were excelling academically and planning prudently for college.

I cleaned up my act just in time to barely squeak by and gain acceptance to University of California, Santa Barbara. Since my grades and SAT scores were not high enough to qualify automatically for UCSB, I received a conditional acceptance letter in the fall of my senior year, a generous offer that the admissions office made after a little persuasion from the cross-country coach. All I had to do to be formally accepted for the fall was to get a B in each of two classes, English and Chemistry, during the spring of my senior year.

English was no problem; it was my best subject. I even crashed the Advanced Placement English exam at the end of my senior year. Advanced Placement examinations are given to high school students in various subjects who have taken an intensive, college level curriculum in that subject for the entire school year. At the completion of the class, students are administered a nationally standardized "AP" exam, and a passing grade earns them college credit and the right to bypass the freshman level courses in that subject in college.

I had not taken the brutal AP English class like many of my academically advanced friends, who were bogged down all year reading various classics and then preparing book reports and taking exams on the material. I checked and found out that it was not mandatory to take the AP course to sit for the exam. I was enticed by the ten units of college credit offered, so I paid my $65 and registered for the exam.

I showed up in the AP English class on final exam day to take the test, having never attended the class before. More than one snicker was heard when the teacher called my name, asked who I was and what I was doing there, before begrudgingly handing me a special test different from the others. During my checking, I found out that there were two types of AP English exams, one focusing on literature (covering all the classics read during the school year) and the other focusing on language skills. I hadn't cracked any of their books so I chose door #2, the Language and Composition exam.

The results were mailed to students about six weeks later during the summer. On a five-point scale, three or better was a passing grade worth the ten college units. To their horror, all three of my close friends taking the exam received scores of 2. They tied up the phone lines for quite a while bitching to each other: "You too? What a rip-off!" When one of them got around to calling me and I informed them that I had passed with a 3, they were livid!

Pulling a B in spring semester Chemistry class was a whole different story. I didn't know the first thing about Chemistry after spending the entire first semester chatting with a girl I liked, Lisa Rosenbaum, who sat next to me at the back of class. This took all of my attention and concentration, but luckily I had carefully selected a "Mick" teacher, short for Mickey Mouse, meaning that the teacher was a little lax on discipline and a generous grader. Knowing which classes were Mick's was invaluable if you wanted to be assured of a good grade with little effort.

The Chemistry exams with my particular teacher were Mick's because every class was given the same test; and when exam time came, I was always able to procure a copy of the test or a least a comprehensive synopsis from students who had already taken the identical test. These investigative efforts usually earned me a solid B. I was so flaky on homework and class assignments I still only had a C+ going into the final exam. I was slightly worried about being on the bubble, particularly since my attention and attendance in class was faltering as I developed a strong case of senioritis with summer approaching. I panicked when I discovered that a special final exam schedule would be in effect which had our class taking the final before anyone. I was doomed!

Luckily I was able to rely on my friend Robert Benun, my bathroom hiding partner on the tenth grade cross-country team and a future triathlon training and racing partner, who was pulling straight As and headed for the University of California, Berkeley. Rob was doing very well in Chemistry, so he offered to help prepare me at the last minute to pass the final on my own. He came over to my house the night before my final and taught me a semester of Chemistry in a four hour cram session! I got an honest A on the final, a B+ in the class, and was headed to UCSB.

5

THE RIDE

February 4th, 1984. My 19th birthday arrived, and by now everyone in Tropicana Gardens, the off-campus dorms where I lived for two years, had heard of my outrageous boast to ride all the way to LA from school—the pressure was on!

According to the map, I calculated the trip to be 104 miles, a beautiful ride through the coastal communities of Santa Barbara and then Ventura counties, out to Point Mugu and down the Pacific Coast Highway (PCH) through Malibu. Entering greater Los Angeles, and the final, daunting 13 miles over Topanga Canyon Road from the beach, I would pass over the Santa Monica mountains to Woodland Hills in the Valley.

I took off early and alone while everyone else was still sleeping off the previous night's partying. My four suite-mates were actually quiet out of respect for my need to get a good night's sleep and the impending effort of the next day.

I dressed in running shorts, a T-shirt and windbreaker, and running shoes. I carried a small backpack with a little food, some money, the route map, and miscellaneous other items. The first 15 miles from the UCSB campus were entirely on a bike path through suburban Goleta that feeds into the streets of downtown Santa Barbara. I negotiated a brief climb up Ortega Hill Road, which serves as a geographical closure to the valley-like greater Santa Barbara area, and descended into the small coastal community of Summerland. I then followed the frontage road of Highway 101, passing beautiful beachfront estates, all the way to Carpinteria, 25 miles into the ride.

I took my first stop, losing the windbreaker, and grabbed a soft drink and candy bar at a liquor store. Soon after leaving Carpinteria, the ocean comes snug up against the cliffs of the coastal Santa Ynez mountain range, with only Highway 101 in between. In the early days, stage coaches were often trapped in this area for days at a time, waiting for the tides to drop so they could travel on the coast road that was frequently underwater. The few pockets of land on this 13-mile stretch between Carpinteria and Ventura are dotted with tiny communities like La Conchita and Sea Cliff. The cliffs and ocean in this area carry rich deposits of oil, and numerous rigs are visible off shore while the hills are populated with oil wells and private roads traversing the cliffs to reach them.

I cruised through the city of Ventura and into Oxnard, about 50 miles from school. I felt fantastic, excited about covering the new terrain. Exploring new territory always helps mask fatigue. The only signs of wear so far were some aches and pains from sitting on the bike so long with uncomfortable clothing that pinched and chafed here and there.

I stopped at a mini-mart in Oxnard. It was getting warm and I didn't realize I was dehydrating—a cool breeze while cycling takes away the perception that you are sweating and losing water. I pounded a ton of root beer and ate some high performance food like a Hostess fruit pie, a candy bar, and some Skittles for the road. Sufficiently fueled and finished burping, I continued through Oxnard and reached a familiar intersection. My old neighbors from Woodland Hills, the Rochins, had moved to Oxnard about five years before. I saw the turnoff to Silver Strand beach and decided to take the two-mile detour to see if they were home and impress them with my incredible journey so far. No one was home so I left my calling card, a Milky Way wrapper wedged in their front door jamb. I would call later and explain while offering proof that I had been there.

The two miles back to my route on Channel Islands boulevard were into the wind, and I felt the first real signs of fatigue. I decided not to take any more detours after that and followed my route through Port Hueneme. Soon I was out of town and riding through the farmlands in an area noted for its strawberries and other crops.

I was quite a ways inland—how did that happen?—I was just on the beach! I headed back towards the ocean and Point Mugu, which marks the beginning of the coastal Santa Monica mountains. At Point Mugu the coast highway meets the ocean again and hugs the coast all the way to Los Angeles. I thought I was heading South at this point as I commonly reference direction by the ocean to the West. But from Santa Barbara all the way to the Santa Monica Bay, the California coast has a peculiar jut in it so that the beaches actually face South, and when traveling down the coast, you are actually heading mostly East.

The eight miles from Point Mugu to the Ventura/Los Angeles County line are completely deserted, just mountains and the rolling hills on the edge of the ocean. The only point of interest is the Great Sand Dune, which rises straight up from the highway for a couple of hundred feet. I recognized it from a camping trip in high school.

Later it would become a traditional rite of passage into the stud training club. Whenever we rode by it, which was always on a long ride since it was so far away, those who dared would dismount and sprint up to the top and then tumble down. Anyone who declined would be ridiculed as a wimp for the rest of the long ride home. I always felt better after a charge up the sand dune. It was an invigorating break from the monotony of a long ride.

County line was the 67-mile mark of the ride and the site of the popular surfer/biker hangout Neptune's Net restaurant. Neptune's Net was the first opportunity for food or water since Oxnard 20 miles back, so I stopped in for a Squirt and some licorice, keeping to my tradition of sampling different high-quality soft drinks and candy at the various stops on the ride. I was feeling some major aches and pains by this point, particularly in my shoulders from the backpack, and my feet were very sore and nearly numb from pushing the pedals for so long in the ill-suited, soft-sole running shoes. I was walking pretty stiffly around Neptune's Net, and it actually felt better to get back in the familiar position astride the bike.

Further down the coast, 76 miles into the ride, I successfully tackled a brutal two-mile ascent on Point Dume. The coast highway at the base of this climb turns inland and is sheltered from the ocean breezes by the hillside. On this February afternoon, with the still air and the sun beating down on me, it felt like climbing in an inferno, and it was definitely the low point of the ride so far.

After several miles of rolling hills, I faced the second toughest climb on the highway, a one-mile grind to the entrance of Pepperdine University directly above downtown Malibu, and the intersection of Malibu Canyon road and the PCH.

I was in familiar territory when I reached the top, having spent many summer days traveling from the Valley to the beach on Malibu Canyon. For the first time all day, I paused at the top to take in the view of downtown Malibu, the Malibu Pier and the famous gate-guarded homes of the Malibu colony. I knew I was going to make it at this point and wanted to enjoy the moment, here at the 83.5-mile mark of the ride.

After a minute or two, I descended down to Malibu and celebrated prematurely with an ice cream cone at Fosters Freeze just beyond the Malibu Pier. I had ridden for 5 hours and 15 minutes. I had left at 8:30, so it was now 2:30, still a good three hours until dark, with only around 20 miles to go. The coast was flat for six miles to the entrance of Topanga Canyon where I would turn inland and climb to the Valley and my home in Woodland Hills. The canyon road to the Valley was 13 miles long, almost all of it uphill with very little break. I had driven it many times but never biked it.

After enjoying my large, soft vanilla ice cream cone with a chocolate dip, I set out for what would become the hardest two plus hours of my life on a bike. Topanga Canyon is a busy connector from the San Fernando Valley to the beach. It's jammed with beachgoers on weekends escaping the Valley heat, and during weekday rush hours with commuters looking to beat the busy 101 Ventura freeway for the commute from the Valley to West Los Angeles. The canyon's namesake is the town of Topanga, located near midway of the Valley and the beach. It is known as the last hippie outpost in Los Angeles. Cruise through the center of town and you will see why; a gourmet natural food restaurant, several arts and crafts stores, roadside stands for fruit, sunglasses and tie-dye T-shirts, a psychic palm reader, and a nudist colony.

The first two miles were a very gradual but acceptable ascent into the canyon, no problem even for my tired legs. Then I encountered what was later christened "The Topanga Wall," a 2.5-mile vertical climb.

At the top the road returns to flat or gradual uphill as it winds through Topanga. Then the incline steadily increases up to the summit, nine miles and about 1500 feet above the ocean.

I somehow made it up the Wall and into Topanga, bike wobbling back and forth and legs burning from fatigue for the first time in the ride. The heat made my backpack feel like I was wearing one of those electric heating pads, and my T-shirt was soaked with sweat along the outline of the pack. I was good on food and water, so I rolled through town and began gradually climbing towards the Valley.

It took a good hour to make it through the canyon, and I paused at the entrance to the "Top O'Topanga" trailer park to enjoy the magnificent view of the San Fernando Valley. Riding time was 6 hours, 40 minutes—I could now smell home! I wasn't quite as exhilarated as when I reached Malibu—emotions were masked by the volume of fatigue I had acquired since that point two long hours ago. I felt jittery and feverish and a little dizzy, perhaps from the sun and a bit of dehydration. Stopping seemed harder than carrying on, since all the symptoms of fatigue hit me when I paused to think about it.

All that was left was an exciting winding descent into the Valley, and a three-mile cruise through the neighborhood in Woodland Hills to home. I barreled down the descent, feeling like a real cyclist and daydreaming about the Ironman. It had been a long, tough day, but I didn't feel dead or anything, just a little spaced out. I did wonder how the hell I would ever run a marathon after a ride of this length.

I turned off Topanga Canyon Road for the final three miles through the foothills to home. The toughest hill remaining was right after the turn, so I stopped for a quick water break at Gary's Market. Leaving the market, I hit the hill and my legs were practically numb. The long descent on Topanga coupled with the water break had caused all the blood to leave my legs, and I could barely move up the climb.

I could feel every muscle group in my legs strain at the task of turning the pedals over. With just running shoes and no toe clips or straps to affix my feet to the pedals like a serious cyclist, my propulsion consisted solely of pushing down on the pedals, my legs acting like pistons. It would have been much nicer and more efficient to have hardsoled cycling shoes strapped to the pedals so I could apply force throughout the pedal stroke in a circular motion. Toe clips and straps also allow a rider to stand up and use the body weight to aid in turning the pedals over when additional force is needed, such as on a tough hill at the end of a seven-hour ride by a rookie rider.

I passed the entrance to Woodland Hills Country Club where I would sneak on the course many evenings to enjoy a twilight round of golf (skipping the holes near the clubhouse). We also used the Woodland Hills course for late night "ice-blocking" sessions with members of the cross-country team in high school. For ice-blocking you buy 25-pound blocks of ice from the big dispenser machines found in supermarket parking lots, carry it to the top of a nice steep hill, then sit on it and slide down the grassy slope for some high-speed fun.

I arrived home a little before 5 PM, covering the 104 miles in a riding time of seven hours exactly. I had carefully stopped my watch at each break from riding as the total trip time was actually around 8 1/2 hours. That night was the traditional Kearns family dinner birthday cele-bration. The birthday boy or girl would always select the menu, and of all the food in the world, I selected my Mom's homemade chili with corn and an ice cream cake. I think the family preferred celebrating my brother Jeff's birthday, because his standard menu selection was steak and lobster.

My family could scarcely believe I had made it, nor could I. Entering the house was when the distance I had traveled really hit me. I had previously only conceived of that journey being possible by car, but now my perspective was changed forever and the UCSB to Woodland Hills ride would become my favorite, to be repeated numerous times while attending UCSB.

Although I had eaten plenty of junk snacks along the way, after showering and unwinding at home, I was famished! I wolfed down tons of chili, accompanied by several English muffins and several pieces of ice cream cake. The wish I made when blowing out the candles had to do with healing my leg, becoming a triathlete, and doing the Ironman.

I was called from the table to take a call from my roommate Ian Gillern at school, inquiring if I had made it. I proudly related to him some details of my journey. He was pretty excited and hung up to spread word all over the dorm. A few minutes later the phone rang again; this time it was a girl I liked, Liz Gilbert, calling to congratulate me—now I was floating! Ian was so inspired that in the coming year he, along with another roommate John Gilman, took up cycling seriously. The following spring both of them completed the same route to my house from UCSB.

6

A DAY OF SPEED

In the spring of 1984 my leg was still healing, and I was unable to run, but I was swimming and cycling diligently. Soon after the birthday ride, my parents went in halves with me on a new bike for a birthday present. I selected the classic celeste green Bianchi model and got outfitted with all the proper gear: bike shoes with cleats to clip and strap into the pedals, helmet, gloves, even a brown and yellow "Renault/Elf" cycling jersey, the same worn by World Champion Greg LeMond and his French professional team.

I got some goggles and a Speedo bathing suit and went to the campus pool to attempt, cold turkey, to swim 2.4 miles, or 176 laps of the 25 yard pool. I completed the distance in one hour and four minutes, not bad for my first time out, and better than Scott Tinley in the previous years' Ironman, according to the splits listed in my magazine article.

Triathlon training was fun! Instead of moping around with another running injury and watching others perform in track meets, I now was on a mission to become a triathlete. I evolved from plain old lap swimming to faithfully doing the interval workouts I read about in *Triathlon* magazine suggested by Dave Scott, like 9 x 150 yards or 6 x 300 yards. I was swimming on my own, but learning to use the pace clock to monitor my interval times, and even getting the flip turn down.

I joined the UCSB cycling team, which was known as a club sport, meaning they competed against other schools, but the sport was not officially sanctioned by the NCAA or funded by the school. The team workouts were my first introduction to pack riding, and right from the start I never enjoyed it. It was unnerving to ride so close to others and have to concentrate so intensely, worried about crashing the entire ride. Since we rode in a pack with others breaking the wind most of the time, the rides all seemed really easy, like we were barely getting a workout. The only time it was hard was when it was your turn to "take a pull" and move to the front of the pack to break the wind for everyone before drifting off to the side and returning to the draft in the back of the pack. I was constantly scolded for taking too long of a pull or speeding up from the constant pace during my pull. I much preferred riding alone or with one or two others, pushing the pace and exploring new roads leading into the mountains behind Santa Barbara.

My first bike race was called the San Ardo Road Race, located off Highway 101 between Santa Barbara and San Francisco in the middle of nowhere. I was entered in the novice division and would race 47 miles, two laps of a 23 1/2-mile circuit course. The race proved that it was not my destiny to be a cyclist. Warming up before my race, I cruised slowly in front of the start/finish line, past the lineup of expert division riders waiting to start their race. Suddenly I lost my balance, and unable to extract my shoes from the pedals on time, I fell in a heap right in front of everyone. Some girl came out of the crowd to help extract me from my bike and get up, and I rode off with my tail between my legs!

When my race started, I was ready for action. In running, a race means pure pain for the entire event, but this is not true in cycling. We started out very slow; it seemed easier than the UCSB training rides. I couldn't believe it—I was prepared to suffer for 47 miles. I asked my teammate what was going on and he said, "just be patient." I was patient for half of the first lap until I couldn't stand it, and I jumped away from the pack and took off alone, just as I saw Greg LeMond do in the video presentation of the 1983 World Championships road race we had viewed at the Wednesday night team meeting of the UCSB Bike Club.

I put my head down and pedaled as hard as I could and soon got a gap of 200 meters or so. I was beaming when I crossed the start/finish line at the halfway point of the race. My smile said, "See, you shouldn't have scolded me for going to the front in training, I'm totally dominating in my first race!" The pack was almost out of sight as I hammered along on the second lap, envisioning victory. I rode the whole second lap alone, and when I saw the two miles to go sign on the road, I picked up the pace for my glorious ride down the homestretch. I felt my victory was so assured that I had stopped looking back after the first lap.

If I had looked back, I would have seen this huge mass of flesh and steel bearing down on me at great speed. No worries though, I passed the one-mile to go sign, then the 1/2-mile to go—I was home free! With a quarter-mile to go I heard a strange noise. It sounded like a wind storm, the noise a pack of cyclists makes when they approach you from behind. They blew by at amazing speed, standing up on the pedals and rocking their bikes violently back and forth sprinting for the finish. I came across in ninth place totally bewildered and frustrated by what had happened. It wasn't fair! I led the whole stinking race, and all I had to show for it was a lousy ninth place.

I only did one more road race that season, mainly to visit my high school buddy Robert (the Chemistry tutor) who had picked up cycling simultaneously at UC Berkeley and now rode for their team. He challenged me to come up with my Gaucho teammates and battle the Bears at the Brentwood road race, a small community east of Berkeley near Livermore. All I can remember is that I placed 14th and had to urinate so bad during the race that I just pulled over and went and then was able to catch right back up to the pack.

As the season progressed without my participation, I became a forgotten member of the cycling team. They were having a powerhouse year and were favorites to win the Western Regional Collegiate Championship—a weekend series of races outside of San Luis Obispo in May, attended by all the colleges in the Western United States.

The events scheduled included a road race, criterium and time trial for both novice and expert divisions. I was intrigued by the time trial as it was an honest, straightforward race against the clock where the fastest man won. I entered.

The day of the championships would go down in my personal history in more ways than one. I barely slept Friday night, in part due to pre-race anxiety but mostly due to our obnoxious neighbors next door on Del Playa road in Isla Vista. Del Playa was the southern border of town and ran adjacent to a bluff overlooking the ocean, so apartments on the South side of the street backed up to the water below and were the most sought-after housing for UCSB students. Del Playa was packed with as many apartments as possible to take advantage of the location, lining the bluff for the length of town about a mile and half. They were built mostly in a bowling alley fashion, very skinny and very long. Our duplex had six bedrooms lined up one after the other, interspersed with a couple of bathrooms, down one long hallway.

The residents of Isla Vista were almost all college students at a school with a deserved party reputation. On weekends, all hell broke loose, particularly in the bowling alleys of Del Playa. Nothing rivaled the annual Halloween bash where the street was closed to host an estimated 30,000 revelers.

One of the party headquarters that year happened to be the apartment next door. Loud music, alcohol, and loud people would emanate from the neighboring apartment every weekend until the wee hours. My roommates and I had several confrontations with them over the year, but it never slowed down the party machine.

The Friday night before the race was a particularly loud and long party. A few shouts of "shut up" were futile, so I just suffered through it the entire night. When I left for the race at 5 AM, I decided to play a prank on them, with little danger of getting caught. I started my car in the parking lot, then ran over to their apartment entrance, dragging a hose up some stairs and depositing the end through an open window into their living room. I turned the water on to a moderate flow and ran like hell to my car and drove away.

I was gunning my Volvo up Highway 101 towards San Luis Obispo, hyped up from the adrenaline rush of the hose prank and of course the impending race. I don't know how fast I was going because my speedometer was broken, but I saw a highway patrol car up ahead and slowed drastically for a long gradual approach from the rear until I was matching his pace. I figured I'd be safe pacing off him so I cruised along with my escort for several miles. Suddenly he flashed on his lights and motioned for me to pull over. He said that he was cruising along at a steady 65 miles per hour, so that I was breaking the speed limit following him! I said my speedometer was broken so I was following him to be safe. No go—he wrote me up for 65 and soon I was back on the road, a little lighter on the pedal than before the encounter.

I arrived in plenty of time before the time-trial, which was a 10 1/2 mile, out and back course over rolling hills in the small town of Rinconada in the mountains above San Luis Obispo. I was so nervous I could barely get my feet in the pedals, and they shook violently while an official held me up on my bike, balancing me before my official send-off time. Once I got going, I felt a tremendous surge of power and absolutely no pain—I was overdosing on adrenaline!

The ability to tap this resource could, in fact, be my primary peak performance asset. For some reason, and without much conscious control, my body is able to rise to the occasion for important events. Even if I've been sick or training poorly prior to an event, I have repeatedly been able to pull off a peak performance and feel fantastic during the race.

What is happening is that the body's adrenal glands are responding to a message in the brain that indicates an impending extreme stress—whether it be a physical challenge like sports or a matter of life or death, like lifting a car to rescue a trapped baby. The adrenal glands then secrete a large amount of stress hormones into the bloodstream. These hormones affect various systems of the body and bring everything to a heightened state to prepare for the impending effort. The symptoms include nervousness, lack of appetite, dry mouth, increased heart rate, rise in body temperature, rapid, shallow breathing, and increased muscle tension

This is sometimes referred to as the "fight or flight response," a defense mechanism that evolved in prehistoric humans to allow them to survive the frequent life-threatening situations they were placed in. Everyone experiences this effect in modern day stressful life. Getting into an emotional or violent confrontation with someone, running late, feeling overworked, getting stuck in traffic, or standing at the starting line for an important race all elicit these fight or flight symptoms as the body prepares for what it thinks is a life or death encounter.

It is known that people with type A behavior who run on high stress frequently overdose, whether intending to or not, on the body's stress response. This occurs when the body is continually placed under too much stress, without allowing for balancing periods of low stress to rejuvenate. The importance of avoiding this overstress is well known, and society has built in customs like daily sleep to balance the activities of our waking hours, weekends to balance the work week, and vacations to balance our home routines. It is very important for an endurance athlete to balance their training schedule and their lives with enough rest and periods of low stress to be able to absorb all the physical stress that training exacts on the body. This principle is frequently ignored by highly motivated, goal-oriented people, and they are prone to crashes in the stress response system where the body becomes exhausted.

The common symptoms of overtraining, or the chronic fatigue syndrome, are often a result of the overuse and exhaustion of the adrenal glands and their corresponding lower than normal secretion of stress hormones. If you overdose on stress, whether it's an enjoyable stress like an outdoor adventure or training and racing, or typical stress like working too hard, arguing with family members or co-workers, or experiencing tragedy in life, the body will initially respond by functioning at a high level, then eventually become exhausted and operate at a much lower than normal level.

For an athlete to be able to control life's stresses, can be a tremendous challenge. But when life's stresses are successfully balanced, the athlete will have a tremendous reserve to tap into when they ask the maximum from their bodies.

Maybe the positive side of my inconsistent training patterns and penchant for low-stress training is that I can tap into a tremendous reserve when I push my body to the edge and ask it for a peak performance. I don't think I consciously wanted to be an inconsistent, frequently tired and broken down athlete, but for some reason I have always been, no matter how hard I have tried to follow a strict schedule.

Early into what felt like the ride of my life, I caught a couple of riders who had started at 30 second intervals in front of me before the turnaround. I knew I was having a good day, but then again these were novice division riders, first-year racers like myself, of vastly differing abilities.

I crossed the line in 24 minutes, 27 seconds, good enough to be the winner of the novice division and the fourth best time of the day overall, only one minute, 25 seconds behind the expert division winner, the fastest collegiate cyclist in the West. My long lost teammates were suddenly my buddies, and they urged me to stay a few hours for the road race. I had no interest in that—they probably figured I could use my strength to lead them into position for victory, sacrificing myself for the team in other words. In fact they asked me to "Stay and race, for the team!" No thanks—besides, I had a date for the Magic Mountain amusement park in Los Angeles that evening with a girl from my dorms, and I had a long drive ahead of me.

I took off from San Luis Obispo to stop at my apartment in Isla Vista before heading down to LA. There I would pick up my date Jenny and head to Magic Mountain. I was still pumped up and flying down 101 past San Luis Obispo when I got pulled over by a highway patrolman again! I was truly surprised this time since I was going with the flow in a large pack of cars, albeit a ways over the speed limit. I felt like I was singled out, perhaps because my license plate read *INAHURI*. Or, maybe the jerk in the morning radioed in an all-points bulletin to be alert for a flying Volvo in the area. Was I just being paranoid? In any event, I collected my second ticket of the day, for 78 mph, and continued down to Santa Barbara and then Los Angeles.

The date at Magic Mountain didn't go that great. It was a little more difficult to relate to her outside of the dorms with no peers around. The exhaustion of the long day had caught up to me, and I couldn't wait to go home and sleep.

We headed for the parking lot around 11 PM, dead tired and our heads spinning from all the wild rides in the park. Then Mr. *INAHURI* wouldn't start. We waited for an hour for the Auto Club repair truck to arrive, only to find he couldn't start it either. After 20 minutes of his futile efforts—and nerves getting evermore frayed—I finally checked the fuse box, replaced a little ten amp fuse, and drove away.

I had to drive Jenny right past my house in Woodland Hills on the way home from Magic Mountain, which is located on Highway 5 in Valencia, north of Los Angeles, to take her over the canyon home to Malibu. I hung out at her house for about 20 minutes and then took off for the Valley at about 2 AM. She lived in a community called Big Rock, situated on a high bluff overlooking the PCH and the ocean. As I sat exhausted at the light at the bottom of Big Rock drive, staring at the empty highway and the endless red light, waiting to turn left onto the

Coast highway, my patience ran out. I looked both ways, and with no cars in sight I turned onto the highway, running the red light, to head home. As I headed east towards Topanga, I noticed a single set of headlights in my rarefy mirror far behind me. Sure enough, they belonged to a Los Angeles County Sheriff and he pulled me over.

Not only did I get ticket #3 of the day, but was also treated to a 30 minute wait before he finally returned to my car with the ticket and released me. I woke up the next morning thinking that the three tickets received in one day had been a dream and had to look in my wallet and see the papers to realize it actually happened.

A few weeks later during summer vacation, I went to fight the ticket I received in Malibu, my argument being I was deprived of my constitutional rights since I was kept waiting so long. On the date of my court visit, I decided to ride my bike from Woodland Hills over the canyon to the Malibu courthouse. I got as far as the door to the courtroom when the bailiff threw me and my Lycra shorts and cycling jersey out of the building due to a lack of proper courtroom attire.

It was a blessing in disguise because my plan B to deal with the traffic tickets worked to perfection. I had received a fourth ticket a month later for speeding in the desert on the way to Las Vegas for a triathlon. At that point, I was at risk of losing my license for four convictions within a year. Since the tickets were received in four different counties—Santa Barbara, San Luis Obispo, Los Angeles and San Bernadino—and this was before the sophisticated computer systems in place today, I devised the following plan: I made a separate request to attend traffic school to clear my ticket from each county court. After attending Traffic School, I photocopied the completion certificate three times, mailed a copy to each court and crossed my fingers. A receipt for completion and erasure of my tickets soon arrived from each court and my clean driving record was maintained.

7

THE WATER PURIFIER, THE TERMINATOR AND THE GRIP

Towards the end of the spring semester of 1984, I began jogging again as my stress fracture gradually healed. The first day back I struggled to complete four laps around the track—it felt like I had never run before in my life! Soon I was up to doing my favorite four-mile loop a few times per week, monitoring the pain carefully and eagerly looking forward to a summer schedule of triathlon racing.

My friend Robert and I corroborated on a race schedule together as he was preparing in Berkeley for his first triathlon season. He had a year on the cycling team under his belt and had experience on the cross-country and swim teams in high school. As sophomores in high school on the cross-country team, he beat me out at the end of the year for top man honors and qualified for city finals. He then lost interest in distance running, became a pole vaulter in the spring and a football player in the fall. He also raced in city finals in the 50 yard freestyle for the swim team.

After school, Robert and I drove up to Berkeley for the United States Triathlon Series (USTS) Livermore event on June 10th. We stayed in our friend Richard Motzkin's fraternity house in Berkeley the night before the race, then drove to Livermore in the morning. The race site at Lake Del Valle featured a nasty climb out of the lake on the bike, while the run was on hilly cross-country trails—a perfect race for me!

I had a great swim and came out in 18 minutes. The ride went well, too, and I had the feeling I was near the front of the 19 and under age group. My leg felt fine on the run and, coming back from the turn-around, I saw a guy heading out whom I had met the day before and was supposedly the favorite in the 19 and under division. I was told this by my high school teammate Todd Pearsons. However, Todd was prone to exaggeration. In high school he used to worship various opponents and psych me out telling me how awesome they were. Then we'd blow them away in the race. I think Todd just wanted some company for attempting fast times—it worked!

Unfortunately, Todd was plagued by severe leg injuries throughout college. Even my running career lasted longer than his—he never ran competitively for UCSB. With a high school mile time of 4:17, he was tremendously talented and had boundless potential in tri-athlon. He was a longtime surfer and competitive swimmer. He dabbled on the bike team at UCSB as well, but he always developed injuries before he could get serious.

It was tragic to watch, particularly when he came to understand that his frequent shin splints were the result of something called com-partment syndrome, a common running injury. Frequently, the success-ful solution is surgery to cut open the fascia sheath surrounding the muscles in the lower leg, relieving the pressure in the compartment that causes the pain. Mary Decker had a much heralded return to champion-ship form after such a surgery.

Todd couldn't afford to get the surgery, so he felt stuck and hopeless about his running and triathlon future. I knew he was a more talented athlete than I, and his predicament inspired me to give every-thing I had to the sport.

Todd was friends with this 19-and-under competitor from Santa Cruz that I would be racing, and he talked him up like he was the next Scott Molina. "Wait until you race Jim Scott, he's so tough, he has no weaknesses, watch out for him." Well, Jim Scott was taken care of in this race; I crossed the line in 2 hours, 16 minutes, winning the 19 and under age group, and the prestigious prize of a water purifier that resem-bled a coffee machine.

Scott Molina terminated the field again under extraordinary circumstances, finishing in 2:04, while his brother Sean was third. Molina exited the water in the lead, only to be informed upon reaching the beach that he had missed the last buoy and he had to swim back out and round it or be disqualified. He re-entered the lake, swam back out and around the buoy, and then returned to shore three minutes and dozens of places behind the leaders. By the halfway turn around on the bike ride, he had regained the lead. Unbelievable!

Seeing him pass in the other direction going out on the run course was an amazing feeling. Here was a true sports legend in action, close enough to touch, and it felt like a privilege to be able to race on the same course as him. I felt that enduring the same test as him made the connection much more powerful than the typical worship of sports heroes in football, basketball or baseball. Their world, their playing field, and even their physical attributes in many cases, are so far away from everyone else's reality that it's incomprehensible.

Their skills can be admired and faithfully tracked for years by millions, but they become almost mythological since they are placed on such a pedestal by society and scrutinized so heavily by everyone through the media. I and other triathletes could respect a performer like Molina so much more, knowing firsthand the dedication and sacrifice required in training to create a champion of his status.

Although he was one of the sport's legends, at the same time he seemed like any of the other racers, hanging out in the park after the finish of USTS Livermore. But when I would walk near him or congratulate him, it felt like I was affected by this aura that made me as anxious and self-conscious as if it were Michael Jordan or Joe Montana. It's similar to the feeling you get when you're tongue-tied trying to converse with an attractive member of the opposite sex.

I was training in Woodland Hills for the summer and found a competitive age-group swim team to train with nearby. I was excited about improving my swimming with a coach. He would critique my stroke at each workout and give me tips to improve my technique. He kept telling me to swim with my arms straightened underwater, I guess because they were too bent. Soon I was dutifully swimming with my elbows locked while pulling my arms underwater. It felt uncomfortable and slow but the coach kept telling me that stroke changes would feel uncomfortable for a while until I got used to it.

The next race was the Las Vegas Olympians Triathlon, a big-time, one-time extravaganza put on by one of the shady race promoters that were common in the early days of triathlon. It featured a $75,000 pro purse and a stacked field. The swim was 1.2 miles in Lake Mead, the ride 35 miles from the lake into downtown Las Vegas, and the run a ten kilometer loop through the streets, finishing in the minor league baseball stadium downtown.

It was a brutal race; the lake was choppy and several of the top pros swam the course in the wrong direction. The bike ride had a big climb out of the lake before descending gradually all the way to downtown Las Vegas. It was ridiculously hot during the run, over 100 degrees, and I was pretty dazed at the finish and near collapse.

I won my age group and was the second amateur, 35th overall. As I was wandering around the finish area, I wondered if it was Tinley or Molina who had won this time. I asked a person who the winner was and he pointed to a skinny guy with these unbelievably cut calf muscles. It was the first time I had seen such definition of two different muscles in the upper calf. "His name is Mark Allen," the guy said. I had never heard of him before, but I learned that he dominated the race. Molina had gotten lost on the swim, lost his chain a few times on the bike, and still placed fifth overall, which was probably his worst race ever.

I'll never forget the shock seeing someone other than Tinley or Molina winning the big showdown in Las Vegas. It was enough to elevate Mark Allen to instant celebrity status in my mind. That first encounter with him was mysterious and ominous—seeing some guy wandering around the finish after the race with crazy-ripped legs, never heard of before, destroying the sport's best. Then every month of that season I would get the new *Triathlon* magazine and read about how he dominated another race somewhere on the globe. His training partners called him "The Grip of Death," a most fitting nickname; "The Grip" for short. It referred to his penchant for pushing the pace so hard on training rides that he caused training partners to take a death grip on their handlebars—anyone riding with him better hang on for dear life!

Mark remained undefeated throughout the 1984 season up to the Ironman, but even his disappointing performance there was legendary. That year he gained a 13 minute lead off the bike, seemingly on the way to victory, only to bonk and dehydrate on the run and struggle to fifth place, the most dramatic self-destruction in the history of the sport. Mark commented that he was so focused on spinning his pedals that he forgot to eat and drink during the ride.

This quote fit well with the public's perception of Mark Allen being an introspective athlete with a penchant for zen-like concentration and preparation for a race. The scenario and his comments about the race made it seem like he was this super human robot who was trained to dominate, but got his wires crossed and burned out on the lava fields—not some guy in great shape who didn't drink enough water on a hot day in Hawaii.

Although I believe his message is sometimes misunderstood since it is much more in-depth than is expected of an athlete, I feel he is an outstanding role model for triathletes. He is always emphasizing the need for balance and maintaining perspective in training and racing, and constantly demonstrates to self-centered and stubborn triathletes that there is more to success than just hammering away in training without paying attention to the consequences or keeping a proper perspective.

The next race was at altitude in Big Bear Lake, in the San Bernadino mountains. I exited the swim portion and was tapped on the shoulder by Robert. That was strange since I had beaten him by four minutes in Livermore the previous month. My swimming had been feeling terrible since the coach had changed my stroke, and now it was apparent in the race that it was terrible. What a bogus stroke tip! I was using my arms like paddle wheels on a steamship, using drag propulsion and moving water in only one plane. This is far inferior to using lift propulsion, where the arms act like propellers and constantly move "new" water in ever changing directions.

In lift propulsion, forward propulsion is applied constantly as still water is continually disturbed, just like an airplane's propeller moves still air constantly to stay in the sky. In drag propulsion, water is pushed backward, then force is continually applied in the same direction to the already moving water, and little additional forward propulsion is generated as the paddle, or arm, moves through a vacuum produced by the initial application of force.

This little tidbit of physical law, combined with the fact that I was swimming much slower than before I started going to this bogus coach and his bogus team, caused me to change back to my natural stroke. After a few weeks of forgetting what I learned, I was swimming respectable times again.

After Big Bear came races in Oxnard, Lake Castaic, and Coronado. I won my age group again in each of them, buoyed by my strongest event, the run. My run split times in each of the races were comparable to those of the pros, and they were getting close to the pace I could run fresh before my injury. At the same time, the triathlon races were really taking their toll and I was getting a little burned out towards the end of summer.

8

BABES, BLOW AND YODOLO

As 1985 began in the midst of my senior year at UCSB, I was seriously considering the possibility of racing as a professional in the upcoming triathlon season. I had moved out of the noisy dorms into my own room in an apartment, had a relatively light class schedule as I finally had clinched my target of graduating in three years in June, and my training was going great in each sport.

One day on campus, I ran into one of the professionals competing on the triathlon circuit named Jim Brady. I was shocked to learn he was attending UCSB since I had never seen or heard of him on campus in all my time there. He informed me that he always trained alone, and I eagerly offered to train with him. He was known as a great cyclist and a pretty slow runner, so when he learned I was on the cross-country team, he agreed to do some run training with me. I asked him about riding together as well, but he declined. He said he always rode alone since no one could match his pace. I asked if perhaps I could just try, no hard feelings if he dropped me, but it was no go.

We ended up running together frequently but only rode together on one memorable occasion. One Wednesday, we both crashed the long ride taken by the cycling team each week, a 60-miler down the coast and back to campus. Jim and I in cahoots were able to push the pace incessantly and make the whole team suffer royally, then disappear into the wide world of the UCSB student body and never show up on another team ride that year.

Based on a lot of solo training and regularly running Jim into the ground, I mistakenly believed that I would be a very competitive pro in the approaching season. I found out it wouldn't be so easy at the first races of the season in April, at the Bonelli Park series in San Dimas, outside LA, and then in May at Bakersfield and the second Bonelli Park Series race. I was 20th at Bonelli Park in April, a pretty rude awakening but not terrible, considering it was my first race in the pro ranks. I figured with a little more training I could move right up, but in May I placed 23rd at both Bakersfield and the second Bonelli Park race.

After a few more mediocre finishes, my bubble was burst, and I quickly lost interest in becoming a pro triathlete. My season came to an abrupt end early in the summer of 1985 as the real world loomed after graduating from college.

After graduation from UCSB in June 1985, my future was up in the air. I did well on the Law School Admissions Test during my senior year and sent for applications to law schools like USC and UCLA. But as spring quarter came around, I was getting pretty tired of the constant pressure of school, having taken a full schedule or more every quarter and attending summer school each year. I had been through a couple of interviews with Big Eight firms (as the eight largest international accounting firms were referred to) and was pretty turned off by the corporate scene. I was starting to realize that the pursuit of material wealth may not be everything I had expected, and I didn't relish the thought of going straight to law school and then spending my life sitting in an office wearing a suit, good money or not.

The accounting firm interviews took place on campus during winter quarter when students signed up for interviews with the Big Eight recruiters. The students would dress in business suits and try to talk a good game with their interviewer. You scored points if you could talk like you knew the industry and the business reputation of the particular firm. It seemed silly to me. As a college student, why should I have a business suit or why should I buy one if I didn't—just so I could wear it to an interview? I'll buy my suit after you hire me, buddy! Meanwhile, welcome to UCSB, the land of shorts, T-shirts, and sandals. And why should I pretend I know all about their firm and the industry when I'm just a college student studying accounting? How could I possibly know anything beyond the stupid glossy PR packages they put out for naive students like me to read and learn how wonderful the firm is?

I didn't fare too well in the on-campus interviews, and I didn't get the coveted "call back," where top prospects were asked to travel to the firms' offices in LA or San Francisco (or wherever they were applying to work) for an extensive day of interviews.

Perhaps I shouldn't have ignored the excellent advice of a classmate, who advised me to ask the interviewer his views on "Senator Dingle's proposal" during the interview. Apparently Senator Dingle from Michigan had proposed some legislation affecting the nature of accounting firms' independence and impartiality to their clients. If passed, it would dramatically affect the industry. Knowing about it showed that you were clued in to the accounting scene. I refused to mention it since I knew nothing about it, didn't care, and couldn't pretend otherwise.

With accounting out, I took a job for the summer selling frozen yogurt and soft drink vending machines with my girlfriend's cousin Richard Rylander. It was a rude introduction into the real world. There was no salary, just pure commission in this two-man show. I would cold call on health clubs and mini-marts, trying to get them to buy a soft-serve machine tied in with a new all-fruit, nondairy frozen dessert called *Yodolo*.

The job sounded pretty attractive because I would be on my own time and receive a $1,000 commission for each machine I sold. My boss Richard and I set a goal for me of one per week, and he asked me if I could live on that! How hard could it be to sell one per week, particularly when I could receive one of Richard's great pep talks whenever I would get discouraged?

After a little training from my boss and mentor, I hit the phones and the streets, calling three days per week for six hours to set appointments for the last two days of the week when I would travel to the location an try to close the deal. I received mostly "no" or "owner's not here" over the phone. Every once in a while someone would say "sure" when asked if I could come over and discuss the "profit potential of your location," and I would book these highly sketchy prospects for personal visits.

When I was really down on the job after several dry weeks,

Richard arranged a meeting for me with a successful associate at his home office in West Los Angeles. He showed me his records where he was averaging 2.3 sales per week. He then went on to explain that this was barely enough money to get by, due to the high cost of... "Babes and blow, man, and the money's gone before you know it!"

After several months of thousands of miles of driving and a grand total of zero *Yodolo* sales and zero income, I decided accounting maybe wasn't so bad after all. I called up all the Big Eight firms asking for an interview. Most of them wondered where I was during on-campus recruiting, but two downtown LA firms agreed to see me, Peat Marwick and Coopers & Lybrand. The latter interview was by courtesy of a partner who was a neighbor.

Peat Marwick scheduled a full day of interviews for me immediately, equivalent to a call back from on-campus recruiting. I guess they were desperate or something, or miscalculated the number of recruits they needed, and by the end of the day, I was extended a job offer to start six weeks hence in January.

Coopers and Lybrand granted me a brief interview, and did not extend a job offer or a call back. I later learned from my neighbor that I was a strong prospect but "didn't know enough about the industry" to be an attractive hire. Maybe I should have mentioned Senator Dingle...

Part of my interview day at Peat Marwick was a lunch with a younger member of the firm. We went to a restaurant in the downtown Bonaventure Hotel. It cost $50 for the two of us and I received some of the smallest portions of food I've ever seen—a microscopic piece of filleted salmon, two or three marble-sized potatoes, a couple strands of asparagus, and a couple slices of carrot. I was starving when I got out of there! My host for lunch couldn't shut up about how cool it was to go out to such a great place with the firm picking up the tab. I wasn't impressed, and I felt sorry for the guy who thought it was a big deal to eat in some rip-off French restaurant.

My job was slated to begin on January 6th, so I had about six weeks to chill. I had spent enough time away from triathlon training during the summer to recover from my burnout and was inspired to pick it up again. I trained feverishly in the mild fall and winter weather in the Valley and enjoyed it tremendously. I was getting in great shape nearing the new year and getting psyched about the thought of returning to the triathlon scene the following season. I knew my freedom and my ability to train well would end when I started my job and I began to dread the date of January 6th.

9

DOWNTOWN WITH THE ABs

Work at Peat Marwick began with a week-long orientation program, and my frame of mind when I showed up on January 6th was of swim, bike, and run rather than C, P and A. Orientation was so boring I could barely keep my eyes open—I knew I was in trouble when I looked around the hotel meeting room and noticed all the other recruits frantically writing notes on all aspects of the firms retirement plan and other riveting subjects.

I took to smuggling copies of *Triathlete* magazine inside my thick orientation binder and reading them during the daily program. Once I was interrupted from the magazine by the guy sitting next to me tapping me on the shoulder. He pointed to the gentleman speaking at the front of the room, a big shot partner in the firm, and said to me with a big grin on his face, "Imagine. All that *power!*" I inferred that we had slightly differing goals for our careers with the firm. He cracked me up again after a review of the firm's elaborate phone system and message center. At the coffee break he made a beeline for a bank of pay phones outside the meeting room. Just as I walked by I could hear him ask the operator if he had received any messages yet on the system. "Uh, yeah buddy, here in your second day of orientation at the firm you have a long list of important messages from *powerful* partners!"

I began work in the audit department in downtown LA. During my day of interviews, I had requested to work out of a Peat Marwick satellite office near my home in Woodland Hills, which they suggested was possible. When I mentioned this again during lunch with my advisor during orientation week, they were much more vague. This meant I would be faced with a brutal one hour commute each way in traffic from Woodland Hills to the office or my current client's job site in the downtown area, usually a bank or savings and loan, the firm's specialty. Unless there was a deadline, we would work eight hour days, plus lunch.

At my first day on an actual job site, when everyone broke for lunch, I left in my car, ran a few errands, and sat in a nearby park to eat my sack lunch and read the paper. When I returned to work an hour later, I was quietly taken aside and told the firm policy that lunches were always taken together with co-workers at the same restaurant, chosen by the senior member on the job site. I couldn't even have my own lunch hour! They would take a good hour and a half or more for lunch, which just pushed back the time we could leave after putting in eight hours of work. They would usually choose some expensive restaurant with small portions like the recruiter took me to, and I'd have to pack my own lunch every day anyway to get enough to eat.

I later learned the reason for the firm policy on lunching together at expensive restaurants from one of the few friends I made at the firm, Chris Zilafro. He was an ex-bike racer who I could talk shop with and commiserate about how much we hated the stuffiness and confinement of the job. Chris said lunches were taken together so that they could bill the cost of it to the client as if we were all talking business during lunch. This explained the lack of concern about costs. I always offered to pay for my portion to whoever whipped out their credit card each day, and I would always get a smirk and a "don't worry about it" in return. "Gee, how generous, thanks a lot!"

I was so motivated to train that I dragged myself out of bed at 5:15 AM for either a run on the cold dark streets through the foothills of Woodland Hills and Tarzana, or an indoor stationary bike ride. I would train for an hour, dress in the required suit quickly, and was in the car with breakfast to go by 7 AM for my hour of hell on the 101 freeway into downtown, arriving at the job by 8. I'd usually get to leave work by 6 PM, when it was already dark, and drive to UCLA for a swim workout or back to the Valley to run at the Sepulveda recreation area. I'd get home at 8 PM, exhausted, grab a quick dinner, and then turn around and do it again the next day.

I was quickly burning out. In addition to the difficult time schedule, the job was less than fulfilling. As the low man on the totem pole, I was basically a gopher for the other members of the audit team. Often they were so busy and frazzled they didn't even have time to assign me a task, let alone teach me anything of value about accounting. I'd sit there and read the sports section, waiting for them, and then get scolded for reading the paper. "Well then why don't you give me something to do?" "OK, wait just a minute, I'll be right back..." When I was given a task, often it was so menial I wondered why I was dressed in a suit—it should have been a cap and overalls. I guess since they were billing my time out at $65 per hour, I had to look important.

One of my most memorable tasks included photo copying a stack of papers, double sided, in triplicate. I stood at the copy machine for an entire day. We had daily time charts to fill out, detailing tasks performed, amount of time spent, and for which client. I filled out my time chart for that day as follows:

Date	Client	Task	Time
Jan 14	Cal Fed Mortgage	made photo copies	8 hours

Another memorable time chart entry came when a huge, 12-inch thick computer printout was dumped on my desk at a job in Riverside. We were working at a savings and loan, and the printout was of every customer's savings account balance. I was told to add up the totals of each page and check them against the computer-generated subtotal at the bottom of each page. "Isn't the computer always right?" I asked. Yes, they said, but we have to check anyway, we're auditors. For two and a half days, 20 hours on the time sheet, I sat at the adding machine adding up bank balances and double checking my answers at the bottom of each page. My major excitement came when I'd get a different total—a mistake! Then I'd go back and discover that it was *my* mistake, re-total it, and come out right with the computer.

The last straw came on Valentine's Day. I was finishing up a job at a bank in the City of Commerce, near downtown LA, and working under a couple of "ABs," which was a parlance related to me by my buddy Chris the cyclist. The initials stood for "Angry Bitches" and was reserved for women in the firm who carried a chip on their shoulder and behaved like they were constantly battling for respect in the old boys club of a Big Eight accounting firm. This was true of course, but I thought they could perhaps get further using a little charm at times, or at least not challenging everyone with whom they were in contact.

ABs were very difficult to work with when you were under them on the totem pole. A typical audit team featured people from various seniority levels, and my co-workers on this job were both ABs who enjoyed using me as their whipping boy. On Valentine's Day—our final day at the job site if we could finish on time—I received a delivery of mylar balloons from my girlfriend Colleen. It was pretty exciting and embarrassing since we were working on location at a busy bank branch. One of the ABs remarked to me, "Oh, how sweet, I wish someone would give *me* balloons on Valentine's Day!"

It sounded sincere and was the first display of emotion and nonbusiness related statement out of her mouth in the entire three weeks. I really felt sorry for her, so at lunch I excused myself early from the restaurant (we were allowed to do that if you had important errands to run) and bought each AB a little balloon and card from a nearby party store. When I brought them into the bank and gave one to the girl who commented earlier, she looked up from her desk, and with a perfunctory smile said, "Thanks. But I hope you know this will have no effect on your P-66 report" (a performance evaluation written after each job by your superiors). Like I really cared about their lousy P-66 report.

We worked like crazy late into Valentine's evening, finally finishing around 9 PM. My dinner plans were already shot when the two ABs rushed out and ordered me to drop off all of the dozen or so file boxes, full of supplies and documents used at the job site, to the Peat Marwick offices downtown "on your way home," which it was not. They bolted and I was left to stuff every inch of my car and trunk full of these boxes, in the pouring rain, drive downtown and dump them off. I finally loaded them all up and jumped onto the freeway and into a predictable LA gridlock from the Friday night and the rainstorm.

The six-mile trip downtown took 45 minutes. I pulled into the parking garage temporarily used by the firm a quarter-mile walk away from their brand-new offices in the Citicorp Towers. The first trip to the building with only a couple of boxes took several minutes and left me, my suit, and the boxes drenched. The night watchman saw my predicament and offered me the use of a dolly, which I used to carry four or five boxes the next couple of trips. On the final trip, the dolly hit a bump and the boxes and contents went flying all over the puddle filled outdoor walkway to the building. I crammed everything into what was left of the rain soaked cardboard boxes and headed up the elevator one last time. I piled the whole soaking heap in the office of one of the ABs and headed back out into the rainy night after an hour of transporting boxes (got to remember to write that on my time chart for overtime). It was now 11 PM. I hoped the ABs had a great Valentine's evening!

The following Monday I called my supervisor to request a meeting so I could announce my retirement from a distinguished career at Peat Marwick. He couldn't squeeze me in until a week from Wednesday, which meant when I finally saw him I would be giving him two days notice as a mandatory (to me) family ski trip to Mammoth Mountain was planned for the following week.

"I've decided to quit on Friday." "Uh, Friday the fourth of April?" "No, Friday." He was pretty taken aback, but said he could possibly shuffle some schedules around and arrange it. *Oh gee, since I won't be here, I would really appreciate it, thanks a lot.*

He asked what I was moving on to and I told him I was going to become a professional triathlete. Surprisingly, his eyes lit up and he asked all about the sport and wished me the best of luck. He even extended an offer to return to work whenever I liked (probably because they had invested so much money training me at the copy machine). Actually, several of my other co-workers I had told my plans to offered similar reactions and were very supportive. Perhaps they, too, felt their jobs were unfulfilling and were glad to see someone get out of there to pursue their dream.

10

RACING THE FREAKS

The Monday after I quit, my whole family left on a week-long ski trip to Mammoth Mountain, located in the eastern Sierra Nevada mountains, the largest ski resort in California. I was overjoyed to be freed from what felt like prison and only a few days later skiing in paradise. A storm passed before our arrival, blanketing the mountain, and we had clear sunny skies and an empty mountain all week for some perfect late season skiing. I was running and swimming in the clean high mountain air in between the killer skiing sessions. The overdose of sunshine, fresh air and exercise quickly balanced out my mind and body from the past three months of being indoors.

I returned home from the ski trip with everything set to go for the triathlon career. I had saved a bit of money from working, cashing in on my Peat Marwick retirement plan we learned so much about in orientation, and my parents agreed to let me live with them, free room and board, while I pursued my dream. I'm sure they figured this triathlon thing would be a one-year adventure, similar to the college graduate who travels around the world for a year before settling down into a career.

I remember a discussion over dinner at a Japanese restaurant with my father when I expressed my intentions to leave my accounting career to pursue triathlons. He didn't discourage me, but he urged me to be realistic about a career in professional sports, something desired by millions and a reality for only a select few. When he was in college, he was a champion golfer able to entertain thoughts of playing professionally, but his common sense and practicality won out and he pursued a more secure career in medicine.

He related a story he had told me throughout my childhood to address my fantasy of wanting to become a pro football player when I grew up. He said professional athletes were "freaks" and that their inherent skills were born to one in a million. Only a freak can make it to the top of their sport, and the rest of us mortals had better realize that and focus on an education. This is a valid statement as the sports heroes we watch on TV are indeed freaks, and no amount of luck or hard work by the average person will produce the attributes that they are blessed with.

My father was slightly familiar with triathlon and the leading athletes, and he informed me that guys like Molina and Tinley were freaks as well, super-talented for endurance events. As he was talking, I was thinking of my run split times in the races that were near the best pros, and the bike ride where I hung with Jim Brady, one of the top five cyclists on the circuit. I knew I was vastly undertrained in swimming and cycling, and I truly believed I could be competitive with the top guys with proper training. I offered a halfhearted argument that these guys just trained really hard, and I thought I could do it too, but mostly I absorbed his message.

We agreed that I would try the sport and full-time training for a while and see what happened. In the back of my mind, I thought this to be a one-year adventure as well, and to think at the time about writing a book about a racing career spanning nearly a decade was something beyond my wildest imagination.

The parental support system I had is very common among up and coming pro triathletes as the dedication required for training well enough to make a living largely precludes pursuing a decent career or assuming other large responsibilities. Most athletes in the pro ranks, save for the top echelon who make a comfortable living, find themselves working odd jobs and living with either a supportive family, in a training camp, barrack-type situation with like-minded and heeled athletes, or with a supportive spouse, particularly in the case of the female professionals. The average pro career doesn't last very long, because most tire of the meager, non-responsible existence and move on to a real job, which usually precludes the serious pursuit of pro racing.

Basically, pro triathletes today are faced with the following options to maintain their career: first, be satisfied with being a triathlon bum, your life revolving around the sport and sacrificing a more secure career. Second, marry someone with a secure career and live a conventional, yuppie-type life-style where the family income is not dependent on triathlon racing, and it becomes more of a serious hobby. Third, go really fast and establish a name and a secure career through guaranteed income from endorsement contracts and prize money for consistent top finishes.

I'd guess that 90 percent of the pros fall into one of the above categories. Some other situations I have seen on the pro circuit include the "I'm a super-motivated, don't need to sleep that much, have a career and can still race competitive as a pro." Or, "I can make decent money in the sport even though I'm not a top pro racer, because I'm such a clever entrepreneur." Or, "I have a trust fund, so what?"

Starting out I figured I could handle a part-time accounting job and still train effectively, so I sent the 'ol resume to several small firms in the Valley area. I figured honesty was the best policy, so I informed each of them of my plans to work part-time and pursue a professional triathlon career. Every single firm I contacted wanted no part of it; they wanted complete dedication to the firm or nothing.

I decided to switch industries and soon secured a prestigious position delivering pizzas at night for the Ye Olde Brick Oven Pizza Works in Northridge. I trained alone and lived a stress-free life, trying to get fit for the upcoming professional racing schedule.

My first race of the year was the Bakersfield Bud Light triathlon in May, site of my 23rd place stomping the previous year. I stepped up to the pro starting line in the 64-degree water of Lake Ming, surprised to see many of the guys wearing wetsuits. I made it about halfway through the two kilometer swim until I was completely frozen, barely able to move my arms and slowly struggle back to shore. Brad Hinshaw, then a top swimmer from UCLA who still holds the Hawaii Ironman swim course record at 47 minutes and change, started in an age group wave ten minutes behind us and blew by me near the end of the swim. I actually thought he was a small boat when I heard him approach from behind, almost running me over in the process!

My ten minute déficit and the fact that I could barely squeeze the bars or feel my feet for the first half of the ride enabled me to place a glorious 26th overall. I knew the result meant nothing and was just due to the hypothermia problems, and I was looking forward to showing my real stuff at the next race, the championships of the Bonelli Park series in San Dimas.

I got to watch Scott "The Terminator" Molina, again at Bonelli Park as he dominated the field even though he was scarred and bandaged from head to toe from a bike accident suffered in the week before the event. I had a strong race, but only placed 14th. This was a little disappointing since training alone I was under the delusion that I would instantly be competitive as a pro.

These delusions of grandeur would happen frequently throughout my career as I have always been sheltered from the training hotbeds of San Diego and Boulder where the pros can bash heads every day and know pretty well where they stand against their major competition.

I'm always optimistic, perhaps to a fault, about my fitness level and my chances in a race. On the positive side, I never suffer from lack of confidence or fear of success in racing. I think the confidence stems more from past successes as opposed to resulting from impressive work accomplished in training.

I have developed a training philosophy that can be described as complacent as opposed to many triathletes that have a work ethic that borders on compulsion. My minimalist training philosophy is quite effective as my body responds well to less work load than my peers. This less-is-better philosophy originates from my running days of frequent injuries and bouts with exhaustion from pushing my body too hard. I have lived with a constant fear of overtraining and burnout ever since. Although I have still plunged into the depths of overtraining, it comes not so much from a compulsion, but the desire to be the best I can and making errors in judgement or being fooled by how much my body can tolerate.

It is extremely hard in a sport like triathlon to balance the enthusiasm and desire to do well with the need for restraint and frequent objective assessments of one's behavior and direction. Part of the difficulty stems from the typical, highly motivated, type A triathlete personality. We are willing to do whatever it takes to succeed, even if it means punishing our bodies. The typical triathlete needs motivation and discipline not to get out the door and train, but to back off from their passion when it's in their best interests.

The nature of the sport, three separate endurance sports linked together to form one personal survival contest, also adds to the problem of training effectively. It is such a daunting challenge that triathletes can overwhelm themselves trying to constantly improve or maintain fitness in each event. The body can only take so much stress until it breaks down. When all the factors are added up—the personality types, the volume of training required, and the fact that training methods and styles vary widely from athlete to athlete—the lines of overtraining are crossed frequently and performance suffers. Realizing the importance of this need for balance and restraint is reinforced every time I get overtrained and have a poor performance, get sick, or otherwise stagnate in my career. Making this mistake repeatedly throughout my running and triathlon career has given birth to my training philosophy as I attempt not to repeat past mistakes.

My results and fitness steadily improved through the 1986 season, and I enjoyed some decent finishes in races with strong fields, like eleventh at the Orange County Performing Arts Center triathlon in Mission Viejo in June, and twelfth at the USTS Portland event in July. Of course, since prize money usually paid ten deep, I had yet to take home a check. This was a major goal of mine as even a small check would have helped my ego tremendously and justified my pursuit of a professional career in the eyes of myself and others.

I was pretty frustrated after Orange County; I felt I had a solid result but went home empty handed. Race winner Scott Tinley took home $4,500, a graphic display of how top heavy my chosen career was.

11

MAC ATTACK AND ZEE TOP TEN

After the Bonelli Park race in May, I approached Tony Adler from Northridge in the Valley, one of the top pros on the circuit. He graciously agreed to let me join him for training, and used Colleen's back to write down his phone number on a scrap of paper in the finish area. We were pretty excited to be associating with a big shot pro like Tony.

Tony is a laid back, former Cal State University, Northridge swimmer, who hails from South Africa. Several of his former swim team buddies were actively training for triathlons. I hooked up with this Valley training group for long bike rides in the inland San Bernadino mountains or the coastal Santa Monica mountains, trail runs in the hills surrounding the Valley, and swim workouts at local pools. It was a thriving group back in 1986, with former swimmers Ralph Searcy, Jeff Thornton, Kyle Herron, and other local athletes like Marc DeLeon, Andrew MacNaughton, and Clay Sherman. The group had solidified via an actual "Triathlon 101" class featured in the Cal State Northridge curriculum, the first class of its kind offered at any university in the country.

The group had a beneficial effect on me from day one as we motivated and pushed each other in training and exchanged and debated training theories and information in the rapidly evolving sport. Among the group I soon became closest to Andrew MacNaughton, who went on to become one of the world's top triathletes for many years. Our situations at the time we met were similar, both totally dedicated to making a career of the sport. Originally from Canada, Andrew entered the sport from a ski racing and cycling background. He moved to Los Angeles to pursue an acting career, which was soon put on hold for his budding triathlon career.

Acting was an appropriate career for Andrew as he turned out to be quite a character. Our first meeting was memorable. I was on a group ride with Tony and the others when I was introduced to Andrew for the first time. We struck up a conversation and I learned that he too was a first year pro triathlete. I had never heard of him, and he was pretty scrawny looking, with unkempt, chlorine-bleached frizzy hair, no helmet, and wearing a baggy T-shirt that flapped in the wind while he rode. He rode a dirty, beat up old steel bike with huge gear bags strapped on the front and back.

Early in our conversation, he proceeded to tell me that Scott Tinley was a wimp on the bike and that he could easily dust him. I was incredulous that he could say such a thing about a legend like Tinley—what an idiot! Although I had never heard of him, we discovered that we had done several of the same races like Bonelli Park and Bakersfield and actually finished very close to each other. I was surprised to hear that he was that "good" and didn't know whether to believe him after all that talk about Tinley.

After the ride, I went home and dug out my file of race results, complete with each athlete's time splits for each event. I discovered that we had indeed finished close together numerous times near the back of the pro field. I scrutinized the splits and discovered that although Andrew's finishes were pretty far back in the pack, his bike splits were among the fastest in the field, actually besting Tinley's on a couple of occasions!

That summer, Andrew proved his cycling prowess daily. He was not an aggressive, hammer-all-the-time type of rider; he preferred to dawdle along at a slow pace until he reached the climbs, where he simply maintained the same speed as he did on the flats. He always looked effortless climbing—remaining seated, upper body relaxed, with no expression on his face. Meanwhile, his training partners would grunt and struggle to keep the pace in the hills, alternating standing and sitting, upper bodies bobbing up and down straining from fatigue.

Andrew favored consistent, high mileage training and set the standard for all of us in the Valley. He rode at least 40 miles each day, mostly dawdling along the flat streets of the Valley, commuting to the pool, the gym, or wherever, to hit 300 miles per week regularly. I struggled to match that work load, but I usually tired, although it helped to have a high goal to shoot for and motivate me when I was feeling lazy.

I held on to my philosophy of avoiding excessive training. Andrew and I would have long debates on the phone and during workouts as to what the best training methods were and our differences in philosophy. We finally realized that both of us were different, and we were able to train together effectively for the next five years until I moved to Northern California at the end of 1990. Our situation was ideal since we could easily corroborate on our schedules without dozens of other athletes to alter our plans or take the focus away from ourselves. This way our competitive natures could be effectively controlled, and we didn't kill each other too often in training as is common in larger groups of athletes, such as the congregations of triathletes in San Diego or Boulder.

We both developed steadily in our first year of professional competition and on the local level started to become pretty competitive. Lake Castaic, the site of my high school triathlons, had a three race series during the summer with a small pro purse for the overall point standings. It was sparsely attended by pros, all of them locals, and I ended up fourth overall in the series, earning my first pro paycheck of $250. At home I proudly displayed my check to my family. It was a great feeling to finally receive a prize in an envelope instead of one more trophy. My dad was really excited and declared that I was truly a professional athlete! He took the check outside and laid it on a table to photograph it before I deposited it in the bank.

The big race of the year that Andrew and I were pointing for was the world long-distance championships in Nice, France on October 5th. We did numerous specific rides in the hills of the Santa Monica mountains to mimic the challenging 75-mile bike course through the Maritime Alps outside of Nice. Our favorite workout was a time-trial up Piuma Road, a five-mile winding ascent from Mulholland drive in Calabasas at the western edge of the Valley, to the top of the Santa Monica's overlooking the ocean and the city of Malibu below.

Time-trialing up a mountain is torture. The incline offers no relief from the constant burn of running the body at its red line, and any increase in pace would cause too much lactic acid to accumulate in the muscles and the rider to "explode" and slow drastically.

Riding hard on the flats is more a matter of concentration as it takes a concerted effort to maintain that red-line pace, known as the anaerobic threshold. (Anaerobic means literally "without oxygen." When the muscles work so hard they can't take in enough oxygen, an anaerobic state is reached and lactic acid accumulates in the muscles due to the lack of oxygen). It's easy to let your mind drift on the flats and perhaps use an easier gear than optimum or pedal slightly slower and more comfortably. On a hill the overwhelming constant is the incline, and with each turn of the pedals the body provides the feedback to let you know that you are giving every ounce of effort you have.

The rides really boosted our confidence, especially after one particular time-trial up Piuma where no less than an authority than top pro triathlete Tony Adler proclaimed to Andrew and I, in his distinctive South African twang, "Hey, you guys are ready for Nice!"

We flew to Nice a week early with aspirations of placing in the top ten. It was our first international trip. Our eyes bugged wide when we noticed top triathletes Mark Allen, Scott Molina, Mike Pigg, Ken Glah and George Hoover at the connecting gate in the New York airport for our flight to Nice. I was too excited to sleep on the long overnight flight, and instead Andrew and I struck up conversations in the aisles with some of the pros like Glah, pumping them for information on the Nice race course and their training practices.

By the time I arrived at the Nice Cote d'Azur airport it was 8 AM local time, and I was a zombie from lack of sleep. We had no contact person from the race to meet us in Nice, no accommodations, no transportation. Even clearing customs looked to be a serious problem as visas were needed to travel in France at the time due to terrorism, and we did not have all of our documents in order.

Luckily Mark Allen and George Hoover were next to us in the customs line and Mark, the four-time defending champion, had someone from the race meeting him at the airport who was able to escort him through all the red tape of customs. The rest of us triathletes schmoozed along like a big tour group, "Yes, we're with *him.*" We jumped on a special bus commandeered for the athletes and all their bike cases, and got dumped off downtown on the famous Promenade des Anglais, the boulevard running along the waterfront in Nice. We had a mountain of luggage and had to find a room, so I consulted my *Let's Go Europe* travel book, and we dragged our stuff a few blocks to one of the listed hotels in the book. Andrew decided that the beds were too soft, and we had to drag our stuff around to about three more hotels until we finally found a suitable one for Mr. "Mon dos est delicate" (my back is delicate).

We settled into the room, and Andrew opened his bike case to discover that the airlines had crushed his bike frame; it was totally useless. We thought back to the baggage claim area, when we heard a sickening sound of crushing metal as the bikes were appearing on the conveyor belt—must have been Andrew's. He plunged even further into a daze and we both collapsed on the beds around noon for a nap lasting several hours. I woke up not knowing where I was or what time it was— jet lag at its finest.

The pattern was repeated all week as we were unable to last through the day without a long deep slumber of a nap; nights were spent wide awake watching television or wandering the streets of Nice. We realized how presumptuous our top ten aspirations were when we encountered a group of German triathletes on the street one night. These guys epitomized the Euro tri-geek look as they paraded around in their loud colored swim briefs and running singlets, announcing to everyone that hey, they were doing the triathlon, and were dressed to race with a week to spare. We chatted with them a bit and as we parted one of them announced in his broken English, "Yes, I am do-wing zee triathlon, and am oping to place in zee top ten." Uh, yeah, same with us, and I guess probably a hundred other guys.

Andrew and I were ready by the time the race came. We were finally adjusted to the local time, and Andrew had purchased a replacement bike at a shop in Nice. The swim was a hectic mass start with about 1,000 entrants for the three kilometer (1.8 mile) course in the Mediterranean. I was swimming in a daze of choppy water and flailing arms and legs, getting pounded by people on all sides of me. I had no idea how I was doing, I was just hoping to be able to get a breath each stroke instead of a fist or a mouthful of water. Midway through the swim

I noticed the distinctive multicolored wetsuit of Scott Molina. "Yes!" I couldn't believe that after the chaos of the start I was still with one of the favorites.

The bike course is the most dramatic in the sport. Leaving the Riviera, we climb up on narrow roads into the Maritime Alps, which are dotted with little medieval villages built in a tight spiral fashion on mountain tops. It was easier to defend against intruders in villages built in this fashion. When taking our preview ride over the course the week before the race, we stopped off in a couple of villages to get water, and it seemed like we were going back in time 100 years. Everything was dead quiet in the middle of the day. The only signs of life were a few people in the tiny village cafe where we got water, a clothesline strung between buildings above the narrow streets with drying clothes, or an old person tending to their small garden on a hillside outside the village.

I noticed none of the above at the faster pace of race day as the entire populations of the villages were on the street screaming as the cyclists flew by. My main concern was keeping my bike upright on the treacherous downhills, which were wet from morning moisture and littered in several areas with loose gravel. It made for a very dangerous course, but also added to the challenge, since I had to practice restraint and maintain intense concentration throughout the ride.

I finished the bike along with Andrew in a large pack, one of my first exposures to pack riding. Due to the huge advantage offered in cycling close behind others breaking the wind, riders are often deceived into thinking they are having the ride of their life and feeling super strong when riding with a pack. In reality they are going fast and able to stay with superior riders due to the aerodynamic advantage of pedaling in the slipstream created by the group.

I took off on the run like a bat out of hell, full of energy and visualizing my entry into the big time with a top finish. Early in the run I caught Glah and ran on his shoulder for a couple of miles. At about seven miles into the 20-miler along the Cote d'Azur waterfront, I became impatient with the pace and actually dropped Glah. What a smart move for a rookie to drop an experienced pro who had been in the top five at Nice and other big races numerous times in the past!

I lasted about two more miles until just before the turnaround when suddenly it was like my movie projector went to white, and I totally bonked. (Bonking occurs when the body runs out of the glucose it uses for energy and the systems quickly shut down, making exercise and concentration increasingly difficult.) It can come on rather suddenly as there I was one minute battling for a top ten spot in the World Championships, and the next feeling dizzy and weak, immediately forgetting all aspects of the race. I was thinking only of getting some sugar into my body as soon as possible. I walked the half-mile to the turnaround where I pitched my tent and camped out at the aid station, swigging coke, water, an electrolyte drink, and wolfing down a buffet of treats only found at races in France—little chocolate candy bars, dried apricots, sugar cubes, figs, and cookies—all going down in rapid succession.

Tons of people had passed me by the time I left the aid station, and although I was feeling much better physically, my heart wasn't in it anymore. I jogged on for a while, wondering if I should drop out and hitch a ride to the finish or plod on, agonizing about how close I was to a top ten finish only to see it slip away in an instant. I decided to wait for Andrew and pace him in. I walked for a long time, waiting for him to come by, but he never came.

I finally drifted across the line in 126th place, losing about an hour from the time I had moved to as high as eleventh before the turnaround. Andrew came in an hour later in 404th place, having suffering a similar fate as me, only at the beginning of the run. I was devastated about the result after all that preparation, but at the same time encouraged to know I was so close to competing with the best.

I had planned to tour around Europe after the race as it was my first visit there. I sent some of my race gear home with Andrew, shipped my bike to the Paris airport to store until my departure from there, and jumped on the train from Nice for a three week whirlwind tour. I hit cities like Rome, Florence, Paris, Zürich, Salzburg, Innsbruck, Munich and Amsterdam. I usually traveled by myself, but at times traveled with some Americans I met after the race in Nice, or visited my roommate Barbara from UC Santa Barbara, who lived in Zürich. My touring mode was to sleep on the overnight trains, arrive at my destination in the morning and then go for a long run to check out the whole city. After the run, I would walk or ride the public transportation to visit the sights and museums, have a meal, and then either stay a night in a small hotel or jump on the train for another overnight ride to the next city. Once in a while I would even find a pool and get in some killer, "swim-till-my-arms-fall-off-because-I-don't-know-when-I'll-swim-again" workouts.

I had figured my season to be over after Nice, but my result left me hungry for redemption and optimistic to hit the few races left on the pro schedule when I returned home. I was able to enjoy my vacation in the meanwhile, particularly since the frequent hard, long runs and killer swims made me feel like I was keeping in shape and then some.

I was running out of money towards the end of the trip, and my pants were slipping off my waist as I was living on chocolates purchased earlier in the trip as gifts (oh well, they'll understand), fresh baked bread from the bakeries, and bottled water. And I thought people were supposed to gain weight on European vacations. My 30-day French visa was about to expire, so I boarded a night train in Amsterdam bound for Paris to catch my scheduled flight home the next day.

At about 2:30 AM, when the train stopped at the Belgian/French border, I was wrested from sleep by a conductor shouting my name over and over. "Key-airns! Key-airns!" "Yeah, yeah, what?" "Eh, le passport, le problem." My 30-day French visa had actually expired at midnight and, shame on me, I was into the 31st day. He said I had to get off the train immediately as I could not enter France with an expired visa. I begged and pleaded and showed him my airline ticket leaving later that morning to the USA from Paris. I thought about mentioning Mark Allen and the Nice triathlon, but for some reason I thought it might not be successful this time. "Look, I'm not a terrorist, I just want to fly home." He would have none of it and ordered me off the train. I refused until he grabbed my bags and threw them out the door, and I had to jump off the platform after them.

I found myself at a tiny train station in the middle of nowhere, deserted except for a single night watchman who spoke little English. He was able to explain to me that there would be no more trains to Paris that day. He suggested I walk to another station where I could pick up a commuter train first thing in the morning. It was a five-kilometer walk, or cinq kilometre ("sonk keelomett") as the guy said, to the other station. I had to carry all my bags—a small backpack and two huge duffel bags stuffed full—along pitch black country roads.

I staggered into the nearly empty commuter station around 4 AM. People started pouring in a two hours later, and I boarded a train full of Belgian workers commuting to Paris. The ticket only cost the equivalent of three bucks, and better yet, there would be no passport control since it was a commuter train. The only problem was that I was running short on time, and I had to catch that plane home since I had no money and no place to stay for another night.

I jumped off the train in Paris and took a cab with my last francs across town to the Orly International airport, crashing to the front of this huge line of people waiting for cabs and jumping in as soon as the cab door opened. I figured I owed the country one as I was continually snaked by natives in every conceivable line I stood in during my stay in France.

I arrived only a few minutes before the flight, quickly got my bike out of storage, and raced to the gate area, lugging all three bags and the bike, only to find another huge line at the security checkpoint to get to the departing planes. Yelling and screaming, I ran up to the front and waved my ticket at the security agent, pointing to the plane about to leave out of the gate. He let me right through without X-raying me or any of my bags (I guess I owed France two cuts in line). A train conductor kicks me out of the country because my visa is two hours expired and then they let me onto an airplane without a security check!

When I reached the gate the doors of the plane were closed, but I told the gate agent I was broke and begged him to let me on since the plane had not taxied out yet. I left my bike with him and told him to stick it on the next plane to LA—I'd worry about it later. He opened the doors and let me on (he was American), and I was headed for home.

12

PICK THE WINNER

I immediately started into heavy training upon arriving home. Some good races were still left on the schedule, so Andrew, Tony and I scheduled a trip to Boca Raton, Florida for the national sprint championships on November 16th. I found my swim and run times to be better than ever, and I quickly made up for my time off the bike by going on the Andrew plan and biking everywhere. We'd take long rides almost daily in the mountains, racing up the major climbs. As Andrew was clearly the best climber, he enjoyed toying with us. He'd often feign indifference and give me a huge lead at the beginning of the climbs, then take off after me. Just as I'd be smelling victory near the summit, he'd catch me and we'd have to sprint it out at the top.

After a couple 250-mile weeks right off the plane from Europe, my biking was back, and I was itching to race. We arrived in Florida to find a top field and a generous purse for the sprint championships. My credit card bills from Europe were coming due and with my bank account empty, I was praying for a strong finish. I placed seventh, by far my best race and biggest check to date, $700. I had the fastest run split in the race, a major breakthrough indicating I was able to compete with the best. Scott Tinley blew everyone away for an easy victory while Andrew was behind me in eighth and Tony was twelfth, all of us in the money.

The three of us then took off in our rental car to tour Florida for a few days. We drove up the East Coast, through all the beach resort cities, went to Disney World and the Epcot Center in Orlando, and took a fascinating tour of the Kennedy Space Center in Cape Canaveral.

During the Space Center tour as we drove across the marsh-lands in our bus, approaching the building where they store and work on the shuttle, we were told that it was the second largest enclosed structure on earth, behind the Astrodome, and had the largest door in the world. It looked like a normal sized office building. Then we were told we were seven miles away from it—it seemed like only a mile! We kept driving and driving and upon finally reaching them, the size of the building, and the shuttle, which was in its launch pad that day for testing, were phe-nomenal. It was a great experience to learn about our space program from a first hand perspective.

One of the best parts of the sport is the opportunity to travel the world and socialize with great people. Professional triathletes tend to be a close-knit group. I think this stems from the large amounts of time spent training together and the mutual respect that develops from know-ing what you have to go through in training to be competitive. It's diffi-cult to develop animosity when the majority of pros train together, travel together, and live and hang out with one another.

At races there is usually plenty of free time, since normal train-ing schedules are halted so athletes can adjust to the race site and rest before and after the race. Usually traveling pros are housed together in a host hotel and corroborate for workouts and course previews, meals, a little tourism, and of course gossip. Since triathlon tends to be an all-consuming life-style, there is typically plenty to talk about and share with your fellow pros; the races become mini-reunions throughout the year as the athletes travel from their respective training bases to congre-gate at races on the circuit.

After the race, the sense of relief and satisfaction from finish-ing, and the break from the normal training, leads to a group of people ready to blow off some steam! I can't tell too many wild stories, cer-tainly nothing to match the tales of revelry and conquest commonly found in the autobiographies of our major sports heroes. No, there are not hundreds of groupies at every hotel and every city, and I undoubt-edly missed out on most of the juicy triathlon stories anyway. My favor-ite times have been spent just hanging out in a different city with my racing companions, many of whom I rarely get to socialize with.

Our time in Florida passed quickly and we flew home Thursday, then drove to Palm Springs on Friday for the next race, a brand new event called the Desert Princess Run-Bike-Run. The course consisted of a 10K run, followed by a 62K (38 mile) bike, and another 10K run. This was far longer than any previous event in the sport of biathlon, now called duathlon, which are races of two events, usually running and cycling. The typical duathlon features two runs sandwiched by a bike ride. The event promoters, Greg Klein and Brenda Clark, offered a pro purse for each race in the series and a Princess cruise to Mexico for the series winners. They were able to lure some big name racers to commit to the series, notably Kenny Souza, the undisputed king of the fledgling sport, and Scott Molina, one of the "Big Four" (along with Mark Allen, Dave Scott, and Scott Tinley) men in triathlon. The race was billed as a showdown since Molina and the other top pros had never raced Souza before on his turf, the dry land sport of biathlon.

Despite the obscurity of biathlon relative to its big brother, triathlon, Souza was a well known endurance athlete and a cult figure to those who followed multi-sports closely. He cut a dramatic image—his diminutive 130 pound frame was incredibly lean and ripped, his long flowing hair made him look like a rock star, and his dress and demeanor off the race course did nothing to dispel that image. He always raced in a skintight swim brief and singlet, the better to display his impressive physique and intimidate the competition.

His running and cycling talents were both national class as he regularly demonstrated in running road races and the occasional cycling event he entered. Whenever and wherever there was a professional biathlon, you could be certain that Kenny would be there and that he would win. He hung out in San Diego and trained with all the big boys on land, and there were legendary tales of him putting the big hurt on the tri boys during training. His problem was that he was an absolute stone in the water and had little desire to improve his swimming, so he would never become a top pro triathlete. He would have to be content dominating his little sport which, fortunately for him, grew steadily through the 80s and 90s and launched him into the mainstream of the endurance sports world.

For almost the entire two hour drive to Palm Springs from the

Valley, Andrew and I debated who would win the race, Molina or Souza. "Sure Souza's the biathlon king, but this is the Terminator he's facing, a big difference from the pro biathlete competitors." "Yeah, but Souza can run a sub-30 minute 10K. He'll be gone after the first run." "Well, look at the distances, they're way too long for Souza, etc." Towards the end of the conversation, growing a little bored with our in-depth handicapping of the race, I wise cracked to Andrew, "Neither of them are gonna win, *I'm* gonna win. Ha-ha!" My realistic goal was actually to crack the top ten and take home a prize check.

Since no one had ever done a race quite like this one, there was tremendous uncertainty among the competitors about matters of pacing and strategy. I made an analysis prior to the race that proved crucial. I realized that we would be running nearly a half-marathon by the time the day was over, so I decided to run the first run at the pace I could hold for a half-marathon, rather than treat it like an open 10K. Hopefully I would be able to hold the same pace, with much more effort of course, during the second run. I guess the other athletes in the race didn't consider this because everyone bolted from the gun like it was an open 10K. I stuck to my strategy and was soon at the back of the pro field, finishing the first run in 34 minutes flat, 24th place out of 27 pros.

I felt totally fresh and was soon passing several of the 10K speedsters in the early stages of the bike. I hooked up with Mark Montgomery and we rode through most of the field by the 20-mile mark. Mark was the winner of the first triathlon I ever did, when I was a junior in high school in 1981. Like most triathlons in those days, the Castaic triathlon emphasized relays, and those who did the entire course competed in a special "Ironman" division. Incredibly, Mark beat all of the relays in winning the Ironman division. Mark remained one of the world's top professionals for nearly 15 years, and is still going strong today, pushing 40!

Mark and I weren't sure of our place, but at the 32-mile mark we saw Souza sitting in a ditch on the side of the road, his bike laying next to him. When we passed and asked if he was OK, he said, "I'm sick, man." We had recognized a few of the other favorites that we passed, and I was taking a mental inventory of who might still be ahead of us: Molina, Tom Gallagher, a pro from Long Beach, and a few others

I hadn't seen yet.

I dropped Montgomery at the beginning of the run. I noticed the press truck full of photographers and journalists cruising along snapping photos. I asked them what place I was in and they all looked at me with a confused expression, one of them finally answering, "You're it!" I didn't understand what he said, but soon I saw Gallagher on the side of the road, one of the many casualties in what was turning out to be a race of attrition. He cheered for me and I asked him about Molina, who he said had flatted and also dropped out. "Oh, I get it, I'm *it*. Wow!" I immediately picked up the pace as the realization that I was *it* gave me a fresh surge of energy.

I always enjoy and run best from the front, running scared. Many athletes prefer to run with others and share the pace setting or have someone in front to focus on and chase down. I hate running with others or having to worry about catching someone in front of me. When leading, I can focus completely on myself and go as fast as possible without distraction, letting the others worry about catching up to me.

My second 10K was another 34 flat, by far the fastest among the field. I crossed the line in disbelief over my two minute victory, my first as a professional and of course the highlight of my career. I soaked up all of the attention from the media afterwards, who wanted to know all about my race, but more so wanted to know who the hell I was!

I returned home still refusing to believe what had happened in the desert. My training was on an absolute high; I could do no wrong and feel no pain. In a sport like triathlon, with all the training time and physical discomfort involved, mental attitude is extremely important and has a drastic effect on the success of a training program. My mental attitude at the time put me in the zone where every workout was great and my confidence grew daily.

A couple weeks after the race, an article came out in *Competitor* magazine on the race with photos of Molina, Souza, Emilio DeSoto, (another pre-race favorite), and me lined up next to each other with the caption reading, *Desert Princess Quiz: Pick the Winner.* The photo was a sarcastic allusion to the fact that I was the unknown athlete who didn't belong in the company of the others. The story described me as the darkest of horses who shocked the favorites. It brought back the memory of the discussion Andrew and I had on the drive to Palm Springs trying to pick the race winner.

The final race of the year was the Penrod's triathlon in Ft. Lauderdale, Florida on December 6th. It was over the now internationally recognized (Olympic) distance of 1.5 kilometer swim (.9 mile), 40 kilometer bike (24.8 miles), 10K run (6.2 miles). The race featured a $20,000 professional prize purse. We awoke race morning to hurricane weather and a dawn starting time. With the ominous clouds in the sky, it was still dark when we jumped into the stormy swells—it felt like I was in one of those old movies, trying to survive a shipwreck in the middle of the ocean. I survived in good position and mounted my bike with the main goal to stay upright during the storm, which I accomplished.

The first two guys to finish the bike were directed the wrong way out of the transition area by some guy in a superman outfit, one of the only organizers left on the race course during the downpour. I started off in the right direction for the 10K and soon found myself in second place behind Andrew, who I caught at the first mile. He noticed that I was going to soon have some company, in the form of Robert Roller from Ohio, one of the mainstays on the pro circuit. Andrew warned me that he was coming up fast, and soon Roller caught me and planted himself right on my back—I never saw him the entire run.

The run was three two-mile loops, and by the final loop I was in severe pain. Pushing through the hurricane force winds on the homestretch, I just focused on the sound behind me of Roller's feet splashing the puddles on the ground. I had to keep telling myself that the pain was worth it as I knew I would be content, ecstatic actually, with second. Hurting a little more for first would be so much better, and twice as much money, $2,500 to $1,250.

I pushed the pace, repeating over and over to myself "$2,500, $2,500" and listened for the sound of his feet, hoping it would go away. In the last half-mile, I gave it everything I had, and finally the sound of his feet got quieter and then faded away. I won by ten seconds, greeted by a finish line crowd of a handful, with everyone else taking shelter from the hurricane inside Penrod's bar at the finish line. At least the ESPN and local news cameras were there to film it! I enjoyed the same routine as Palm Springs, talking to the press and explaining who I was. I was also smiling about the $2,500, which would seal my plans to live simply and train through the winter, keeping my career alive without having to go back to work full-time.

I waited with great anticipation for the 11 PM news, which had promised coverage of the race. The sports anchor set the dramatic stage of the triathlon in a hurricane, and then cut to me charging down to homestretch to victory. Because I was in such a daze at the end of the race, I forgot what had happened next. After crossing the line, the camera showed me staggering through the finish chute as a volunteer came running up to me, attempting to pull my race number tag off the front of my shorts as they do to all finishers. She reached out and took a mighty pull in the vicinity of my number and got a hold of my shorts as well, pulling them right down to my thighs. They popped right back up, but the damage was done. The newscaster had seen the footage before and milked it well. "Watch what happens after Kearns crosses the line. Here comes a volunteer; and there go his shorts!" He continues, laughing hysterically "Here he wins the whole triathlon and what does he get? His shorts pulled off at the finish!" The other news anchors were all cracking up, wisecracking about the incident. Then it was on to weather. It was slightly amusing, but mostly embarrassing, bursting my bubble a little bit and keeping me from getting too big of a head.

After Penrod's, things were starting to change for me as word was getting around about this Brad Kearns guy. Prospective sponsors were actually calling me! Some were the same people who had ignored me and my meager resume requesting sponsorship the previous summer. One of them was Oakley sunglasses, the leader in the industry and the brand I had used all year at my own expense. I was kind of bummed when I couldn't get one free pair out of them, so before Desert Princess I peeled the Oakley decal off the front of my pair and lettered my own "Bradley" in its place. A photo came out in *Competitor* magazine showing me close up on the bike ride, prominently featuring the Bradley Oakley glasses. I signed on the dotted line with Oakley when they called and agreed to no more alterations of their logo.

13

KING OF THE DESERT

January 10th, 1987 was the date of the second Desert Princess series race. There was plenty of speculation in the article covering the first race about whether I was a flash in the pan or not. This attention and expectation was a bit stressful since it was so new to me, but hey, I was in the zone and could do no wrong in training. I was able to sit back and enjoy the attention while diligently going about my training schedule.

The weekend after Penrod's, Andrew and I traveled down to San Diego to run 20 miles of the San Diego marathon as a workout. We had no place to stay, but I told him we could stay with some friends. We registered for the race. I then called up a girl I had dated briefly my freshman year at UCSB, Tracy Dunigan. We got along great back then, but had drifted apart as she later left UCSB to study in Ireland, and I had only visited her a couple of times in the ensuing years on trips to San Diego.

I called her home and spoke to her mother, not even knowing if she still lived there. I introduced myself as an old friend wondering of Tracy's whereabouts, and she replied, "Tracy will be home at 6:30." I said thanks and hung up. Then Andrew proceeded to talk me into showing up at her house to surprise her at 6:30. I was nervous since I hadn't seen her in a while and always had feelings for her, unlike other ex-girlfriends which had been pretty much closed books at the time of parting.

We showed up and Tracy soon invited us to stay overnight, so that problem was taken care of. I ended up going out with her and her friend Laura Lovett to a local bar called the Belly Up until 2:30 AM.

Andrew stayed home and slept; we both made the 5:30 AM wake up call for the race. Despite my lack of sleep I was pretty wired since the night had gone very well with Tracy—all the old feelings from freshman year returned immediately. I cruised the 20 miles at a six minute pace, finishing in two hours, a great workout. I stayed up the following night talking with Tracy until 2:30 AM again. When I returned home, I was in love.

The moment that symbolized my new status as a competitor came when I registered for the race at the Desert Princess hotel the day before the race. I opened up my registration packet and discovered I was given race number one. I guess I deserved it since I had won the first race, but it was still a shock. Although the attention I received upon arrival at the race site was overwhelming, I was ready for the pressure and for the race, in the best shape of my life.

My frame of mind for racing was sharper than ever, in part due to a special person I met cycling on the roads in the Santa Monica mountains back in November. His name was Johnny G., a South African native and ultra-marathon cyclist who was training for the Race Across AMerica, the RAAM, a nonstop bike race from coast to coast scheduled for August. He was working as a personal fitness trainer in Century City, and we encountered each other one morning on Mulholland Highway. We immediately struck up a conversation that soon drifted out on various tangents related to his eccentric philosophies of training and life.

Johnny is a unique person and an extremely focused athlete as is necessary to prepare for a race as daunting as the RAAM. He is prone to extremes in everything he does. Once on a ride with Andrew, Johnny and others, Johnny and Andrew got into a heated debate related to some extreme proclamations Johnny was making regarding training and diet. Andrew responded with the question, "Haven't you ever heard of the saying, 'Everything in moderation?'" Johnny responded with an impressive tirade mocking the concept of moderation. "Oh, yes. I wish to train *moderately!* I would like to finish my race in a *moderate* time! I wish to live a *moderate* life and do nothing extraordinary!"

Johnny and his strong personality is not for everyone, but he is a very generous and caring person, a tremendous inspiration to his dozens of private training clients and anyone else who comes in contact with him. An example of his generosity came on our first ride when

Marc DeLeon, who was riding with me that day, flatted and had no spare tire. Johnny offered Marc, who was essentially a stranger, his $80 sew-up spare tire so he could get home.

We became friends immediately and started training together as he was living only a couple miles away from me in Woodland Hills. He turned me on to the latest concepts in training and nutrition, introducing me to various performance nutrition products, a strict vegetarian diet ("Bradley my boy, why would you want to eat something that is dead?") and heart rate monitor training. He went out of his way to help me in any way he could, providing me with some of his extra clothing, equipment and nutrition products, and took an active interest in my budding career.

He even got me started in the personal training world, handing a couple of his clients over to me while he lightened up his work load to prepare for RAAM. He set me up with an agent, his wife Debbie, to handle the increasing sponsorship interest I was getting. She ended up not working out, alienating several potential sponsors until we parted. They ended up divorced soon after!

Johnny had a private gym in Century City where I would train his clients, and we would often meet to go for rides. One night in late December, he put me through a session of meditation and visualization to help prepare me for the race. He turned out the lights and cranked up some dramatic new-age instrumental music. He took me through the entire race, visualizing in detail each segment of the course. It was very relaxing and moving for me and helped to focus on my own performance, instead of worrying about everyone's expectations or what Souza and Molina were going to do to the guy who crashed their party.

Johnny covered every detail, all the way down to my finishing time, which he had me visualize as 2 hours, 38 minutes, 44 seconds. Johnny was prone to preposterous statements related to specific numbers like, "I get a second wind on long rides, usually between 3 hours 53 minutes and 4 hours, 18 minutes." Thus, I didn't think much of his time prediction that he had obviously pulled out of a hat, particularly since it was five minutes faster than my winning time at the race of my life in November. Nevertheless, I was inspired from our session and went out a couple days later on New Years Eve, ten days before the race, and hammered a solo 140 miles across the Mojave desert, feeling fantastic the entire way. I knew I was ready for the race.

On this trip to the desert, instead of Brad and Andrew staying at a fleabag motel in downtown Palm Springs, I had a complementary room at the luxurious Desert Princess resort right at the race start/finish. Along with Andrew, I was accompanied by Tracy, my mother Gail, and two friends from high school, Holly and Melissa. There were also numerous people I had met at the first race or that weekend in the hotel who were suddenly my pals and rooting me on for another upset.

Even the athletes were treating me differently as if my performances had suddenly made me one of the gang. Many of them I had met over the course of my first competitive season, paying them the utmost respect as I was a struggling little rookie pro. As with Ken Glah on the airplane to Nice, I would pick many of their brains for the inside scoop on training and racing and matters of money and sponsorship. I remember a conversation with one well-established pro while we were kicking back at a condo I shared with him at a race in 1986. "So who are your sponsors?" I asked. "I have a lot of sponsors." "Do you like, get money from them and stuff?" "Yeah." (Awkward pause in the conversation. I guess he's not going to elaborate.) "So like, what's the bike course like in Nice, is it like brutal or what?" "Oh, not really, all the climbs are big ring." (Meaning the notorious climbs in the Alps were so easy that he could negotiate them without even shifting into the easier gears on his bike, staying in the big chainring. This was a blatant fabrication, but don't think I wasn't thinking of his boast and feeling insecure as I struggled over the course for the first time during the preview ride the week before the race. Then here was the same guy coming up to me at the bar at the awards ceremony after the Penrod's race, "Hey, buddy! Congratulations! Awesome race, you're really running well. Have you been putting in some big miles or something?"

Another fond memory came with a locally competitive pro in the LA area, whom I solicited swim lessons from while working nearby the pool he coached at in the Peat Marwick days. He had won a few local events, so I asked him all the requisite questions about training and life as a pro triathlete. He ate it up and launched into a memorable sermon, which I related humorously to many of my future training partners. I titled the sermon "pro and pseudo-pro." When I asked him about his training regimen, he methodically climbed down off his guard tower and walked over to the lane I was swimming in, towering over me as I looked directly up at him while submissively treading water.

"Well, training-wise, there's pro, and there's psuedo-pro. Now, pro, you're talking about 25 grand in the pool (25,000 yards per week), 500 on the bike (500 miles per week—probably only Molina and Tinley were capable of this insanity), and 75 running (more than I had ever done in my best week strictly as a runner). Then there's psuedo-pro. Psuedo-pro, you're talking about 15,000 in the pool, maybe 250 on the bike, maybe 40 on the run."

I was totally intimidated by those inconceivable totals, which I guess was his intention. I didn't even think I could make the "psuedo-pro" cutoff. Later in the year after I had turned psuedo-pro, I encountered guess who during the bike leg of the Castaic triathlon. As I caught him from behind and passed him, I couldn't resist saying, "well, there's pro, and there's psuedo-pro."

The gun went off for the Desert Princess Run-Bike-Run race #2 on the cold desert morning. There was snow visible on the peaks high above the Coachella Valley floor, but it was certain to warm up by the time we hit the second run near midday. The second run was over the same course as the first, a couple miles of pavement, followed by a grueling three-mile stretch of a bumpy, sandy dirt road along a levee, and finally returning to pavement for the final mile into the hotel parking lot. Running with fresh legs on the first run, the levee section is slightly annoying but not too much trouble. Footing is pretty difficult, but with all the strength in your fresh legs any missteps in the sand are easily negotiated and the section is over before you know it, completed at a slightly slower pace than running on pavement.

The second time through is an entirely different story. After at least two hours of hard racing (for the leaders), everyone's legs are wobbly, and running smoothly even on pavement is difficult. When the dirt section is reached, it feels like running in quicksand during a major earthquake. A slight misstep on a bumpy section causes your whole body to go flying sideways in midair, and the main challenge of the day instantly switches from going fast to keeping your feet under you. The sand, only a minor slowdown earlier, now provides the sensation that you are running in place.

Joel Thompson, for years one of the world's top duathletes, always had difficulty on the Desert Princess course. Race after race he would be featured among the favorites, set a fast early pace, and then die somewhere out on the final run. He would DNF (Did Not Finish) or shuffle, far off the pace. During an interview after one disappointing Desert Princess effort, he referred to the difficult part of the second run course as the "Dirt Road from Hell," and the nickname stuck.

During the first run, I found myself near the leaders, instead of the stragglers as in the first race. It felt like I was floating, with no discomfort whatever. Midway through the run, I looked over at Mark Montgomery and asked him, "Are we going faster than the first race?" His face was flush from the effort and he could only nod yes to my question—guess so! I came in at 32:30, one of my best 10K times ever, even on the difficult course and leading off a long race.

This easy, relaxed feeling continued on the bike ride. I blew by everyone who had beaten me on the first run and caught Souza in the lead at eight miles. We rode side by side briefly until I looked over at one point and discovered he had suddenly disappeared behind me. I got another burst of energy and disappeared into the desert, the race essentially over at the halfway point.

Even with a huge lead, I was so excited I flew through the final run, and the Dirt Road from Hell, in 33:30, finishing five minutes up on the field. My official time was 2 hours, 38 minutes, 46 seconds, only two seconds off the time Johnny had predicted! I called him and left a phone message, telling him that he was right about my place, but wrong about my time. Two seconds off in fact. I was able to focus perfectly for the entire race, just as I visualized, staying in the present moment and not getting distracted with thoughts of other competitors or slowing down from my pace. Days like these are so rare for an athlete; I enjoyed it to the fullest.

My head was starting to swell from the continued attention and the realization of things like people staring at me and whispering when I was at the hotel pool hanging out after the race. Tracy, Holly, Melissa, Andrew and I celebrated at a local night club, which honored my presence with complementary champagne and an introduction on stage. When I dropped Tracy off in Cardiff Sunday night, it seemed like the whole weekend had been a dream.

The race article in *Competitor* magazine was entitled *King of the Desert,* something my uncle Jack, who was vacationing in Palm Springs at the time of the race, still calls me eight years later! The theme of the article was that I had evolved from a flash in the pan to a legitimate contender. Scott Molina's expert opinion was solicited on the validity of my victories, and he offered the following quote which was highlighted in large type in the article, "If he wins again, he'll be pukin' at the finish line." Pretty heavy stuff for me to read from my hero, someone who two years before I was in awe of just to walk near at the USTS Livermore race. His assessment was correct though. If it wasn't he who would personally be gunning for redemption, certainly Kenny Souza would be.

Molina was still and would always be the Terminator, despite showing poor form in some off-season biathlons. In Kenny's case, these races meant everything as they were the biggest thing in the biathlon world, a world he previously had owned. His two dismal races in a row had many people questioning his reign over the sport. He was not likely to give it up without showing his real stuff, and he was bound to have something more up his sleeve come the February championships.

14

THE EDGE, THE BARS AND KENNY KABOOM

All the attention I was getting over the winter was overwhelming me and I was having trouble training effectively and focusing on the late February championship race. I was forcing myself to have good workouts instead of them happening naturally as they had over the previous months. I was starting to get tired and overtrained from forcing the workouts. Consequently I would miss workouts, which caused me to grow nervous and anxious and feel the tremendous pressure of the upcoming race. I went to Palm Springs for the race with a cold and feeling sluggish the entire pre-race week. This time around, all the attention I received at the hotel was unnerving instead of enjoyable. People kept asking me, "So, are you gonna win again Brad?" I'd think, how the hell should I answer a dumb question like that? It just pissed me off when, of course, it was meant to be supportive.

I did have a secret weapon, courtesy of Johnny G, that I was eager to unveil in the championships. Little did I know that it would make triathlon history and soon totally revolutionize the world of cycling aerodynamics. My secret weapon was a strange looking set of handlebars that Johnny had procured from an inventor who worked for Scott USA, a manufacturer of ski equipment. The inventors name was Boone Lennon, a competitive ski racer turned cyclist. He invented a pair of handlebars which put the rider in an aerodynamic position similar to that of a downhill ski racer, with the hands and arms out in front of the body and pinched close together to slice through the wind. To achieve this position on a bike, the new Scott DH (for down hill) bars had the rider's elbows resting on little pads on what would be the top of a normal bar, then the bars extending out far in front of the bike and coming together at the ends, so that the hands, arms, and elbows were pinched together and extended in front of the body.

Johnny had seen the bars and met Boone at a convention, and being the type that was willing to try anything, ordered a pair to test. I laughed the first time I showed up at his house for a ride and he had the strange looking contraption on his bike. He loved them and was soon bugging me to try a pair. Johnny suggested so many "quite fantastic" things that I had to filter what might be useful for me, and in this case I was content to stick with my regular bars. It was an easy choice since there was absolutely no one riding this new invention, nothing written about it, and was such a radical change from the standard handlebar of the last 80 years.

Johnny continued to rave about the bars on our training rides, so I spoke to Boone Lennon on the telephone, read his promotional material, and my interest was piqued. Soon I received one of the first Scott DH bars, hand made by Boone in his garage in Sun Valley, Idaho. I had to get the bike shop to switch them with my existing bars, and by this time we were into the final week before the race. As is often the case with bike repairs, there were complications with the installation, and the bike was finally ready to go the day before I was to leave for Palm Springs. I rode 15 miles with them in Los Angeles, felt pretty comfortable, and so there they were on my bike at the starting line of the Desert Princess World Championships.

Everyone who saw the bars just laughed or ridiculed them. They probably thought I had just gone off the deep end trying to get psyched up for the race. No one had any inkling of what a tremendous aerodynamic advantage they provided, or that they would spread like wildfire around the world as every serious triathlete had to have a pair to be competitive.

When the championship race began, my legs felt like lead on the first run, completely opposite from the January race. I was left far behind the leaders right from the gun which caused more panic and tension. The size of the crowd, the size and quality of the field, with additions like Scott Tinley, Mike Pigg, and Australian champion Greg

Stewart, and the intensity of the race had picked up tenfold from the previous two races. I knew the sizzling pace on the first run was a product of all this, and I would have felt fine if I had been slowing my pace to stick to a plan. This time I felt terrible and was struggling to run slower than the effortless faster pace of the previous race.

I continued to feel sluggish starting the bike ride, and wasn't blowing by anyone on this day, just lingering at the back of the pack. I could feel my dream of winning slipping away and started to feel sorry for myself there in the middle of the Desert Princess World Championships. Just then my wise-guy training partner Andrew blew by me from behind and offered the following words of encouragement, "Hey, are you in this race?" It totally pissed me off and lit a fire under my butt to chase after him. I got down in my new Scott DH handlebar position and hammered up the road, chasing him with all my might for the next 15 miles, and passing most of the field en route. Souza was finally showing his stuff and was way off the front with the race in the bag. I finally caught Andrew on a long downhill at the 22-mile mark and asked him if he was in the race. We rode the final 16 miles side by side; with three miles to go, we caught Scott Tinley and moved into the top five.

Andrew kept looking over at me and my funky position saying, "God, you look comfortable!" It was true, the stress of supporting the upper body is removed with DH bars because you are basically leaning on your elbows while riding. The aerodynamic advantage is readily apparent as the rider cuts a much narrower profile into the wind with the arms together and forward. With the regular handlebar position the chest and arms form somewhat of a parachute as air hits the chest and has nowhere to go. Now I was slicing through the wind, and through the field as we reached the end of the bike ride.

I started the run in fourth place, soon catching and running with Pigg in third. My fatigue from early in the race had disappeared and Pigg and I were flying. He dropped me at five miles and we finished third and fourth respectively. I was only 24 seconds out of second place but four minutes behind the amazing course record performance of Souza. I had the second fastest bike and fastest final run splits, but my slow start ended up costing me.

Souza proved that he still ruled the sport, and just as we all suspected, when he was on, no one could touch him. The nature of Kenny's career has always been volatile—when he's on, he blows everyone away, but when he's not, he totally explodes and is way off the back. Looking at his record, there aren't too many seconds, fourths or fifths, just a ton of wins mixed with a few DNFs, 17ths, 54ths, and the like. This trademark caused Andrew one day to nickname him Kenny Kaboom—either he blows the field away or explodes trying. It was our private nickname for him for years until one day I related it to a journalist. The next month's cover of *Competitor* magazine was a photo of Kenny winning a race and a two word headline—*Kenny Kaboom!*

I easily won the Desert Princess series title, which accumulated the times of all three races, and a week long Princess cruise to Mexico. I proudly presented this as a gift to my parents, a small way to repay them for all the support they had given me throughout my life and in getting started in my career. I guess my dad could now bestow upon me the ultimate honor of being a freak too, particularly since I had finished ahead of his previously discussed freaks, Tinley and Molina.

It was a tremendous relief to have turned in a respectable performance, under the glaring spotlight, in a much stronger field than the first two races. I didn't realize until after the race how nervous I was about simply finishing and not falling flat on my face. I had a huge lead of eight minutes going into the final race in the battle for the overall title and the cruise, and I kept having this vision that I would flat or break my bike in the championships and lose the series title that was gift wrapped for me.

It was also a relief subconsciously to have not won the race. I think it would have been too overwhelming to have won again and I don't think I was ready for that situation at that point in my life. Instead I was let down to earth rudely by Kenny Kaboom and the others and given a perspective adjustment on my career, that it was not going to be that easy forever. I was now free to prepare for the 1987 triathlon season as a new guy to watch as opposed to facing the mounting pressure and expectation over the next few months if I had remained undefeated over the whole winter and spring.

After the race, Molina came over to my condo adjacent to the hotel where I was joined by ten or so friends who had watched or raced.

I guess it was quite a shock to see him walk through the door, and everybody froze when he wandered in with a beer in his hand. Everybody except my friend Steve Kobrine, who was on a couch with his back to the door, giving everyone a blow by blow of his five hour race. Soon he realized no one was listening, just staring past him at the door. He turned around and jumped about three feet when he saw Molina!

Scott made a wisecrack about the bars when he saw my bike in the hall of the condo. I took him into a back bedroom and painstakingly related all of the information that I had received from Johnny G and Boone Lennon, demonstrating the benefits of the position while sitting on my bike. When we walked out of the back room, he had Boone's phone number and soon had his own set of bars.

Andrew was sold simply by riding with me at Desert Princess and noticing my comfort level. He got his bars, then went on his seven-race win streak. His first win of the streak, and of his career, came in April at the Crawfishman half-Ironman in Louisiana. He thus became the first multisport athlete ever to win a race on the bars, his claim to fame next to mine of being the first to use them. He put four minutes into Mike Pigg from the bike turnaround to the bike finish as they encountered a stiff head wind coming home. Mike's first words when he saw Andrew at the finish after the race were, "Where did you get those bars?" Mike soon had his pair and was off on a win streak of his own, buoyed by his incredible bike splits. It didn't take long for the entire triathlon world to notice this huge technological advancement and soon the bars were in great demand and being used by every top competitor.

After the Desert Princess race, I signed an agreement with a new clothing company called Edgewear, who had been courting me since my victory in January. Edgewear was started by two former UCSB students, Troy Hoidal and Steve Wegner, successful office machine salesmen who decided to venture into the clothing business with no prior experience. At our first meeting, they took an immediate liking to me and vice versa. They were confident and hip, with big dreams about taking the endurance sports' world by storm with their innovative clothing line. They liked my image as the up and comer surprising the big guys, a parallel of how they envisioned themselves in the competitive clothing industry.

After only a month or so of discussions, they were ready to sign me to a contract for the length of my career and give me a small percentage of the company, so I would profit along with them as the company grew. I was very flattered and was eager to "get the Edge" and begin a long relationship with a stake in the business.

The early clothing samples they showed me were fantastic, there was nothing in the stagnant, neoned-out industry remotely like it. Their designs and colors included borrowings from the Native American culture, drawings of arrowheads or birds on a backdrop of soft southwestern pastel colors. Other designs featured nostalgic beach and surfing scenes.

Troy and Steve were pretty pumped about the February race, where I would be debuting the Edgewear clothes. They and some other Edge buddies were all at the starting line in Palm Springs, and although I enjoyed and was excited by their presence, it added to my pre-race tension. After the race I was apologetic to them for not performing better. They were supportive and reaffirmed their belief in me and that they were in this business, and with me, for the long term.

I happily signed the agreement with Edgewear, and then they spontaneously floated me a $250 check as a bonus for my performance in the race. We all went out to celebrate, at least a dozen of my family and friends, and the Edge boys picked up the tab.

Everyone was pretty impressed with my new sponsors. When they met Andrew and our training partners Tony and Clay after the race, they immediately offered all of them clothing sponsorships, telling them to just come down to the warehouse and pick up whatever they want!

It was a great feeling to have such a generous and supportive sponsor. An athlete faces so much rejection knocking on these doors, it's very difficult at times to not take things personally. A resume is basically a measure of one's worth as an athlete, and when people turn it down or ignore it, it feels like a slap in the face. Then you have to show up at a race and see other athletes with hot new bikes, shoes, glasses, or whatever coming out of their ears. It's difficult not to feel envious.

As my career has evolved over the years, I have gone the full circle with sponsors, from being ignored by them, being wooed and sought after, feeling unreasonable pressure and expectations, and being lied to and embroiled in financial disputes with them. For the most part, sponsors provide me motivation and support that has a positive effect on my career. To get paid to use someone's product or just get it for free bolsters my self-worth as an athlete and increases my sense of responsibility towards my career, my public image, and to the companies that sponsor me.

With these relationships, the sport becomes more like a business and some of the spontaneity and joy is removed. I feel it is more than a fair trade-off for having the opportunity to make a living at something I love. Every time I feel frustration from my obligations or relationships with my sponsors, I think back to racing and training in obscurity, totally ignored and unsupported. Nothing is tougher than going it alone, and for every pro athlete who complains about their situation, there are probably hundreds of struggling athletes who would give their right arm to trade places.

That's why as an athlete in an individual sport, I am so disgusted by the major team sport players who expect to be treated like royalty simply by virtue of their athletic status. Luckily triathlons are pretty obscure, so it's hard to find triathletes who have grown too big of a head. As a consequence, the athletes, sponsors, race organizers, media, and everyone closely involved with the sport are on pretty comfortable terms with each other.

15

STOP THAT PLANE!

The first few races of the 1987 triathlon season were up and down, and at the first triathlon of the year, race #1 in the low-key Bonelli Park series, I placed an atrocious sixth, far behind the surprise winner Andrew MacNaughton! I was finding out what it was like to overtrain and my body was still reeling from a hard winter of training and racing, and dealing with all the stressful, yet positive, changes in my life.

The flip side of being able to concentrate and focus completely on the sport and have all the time in the world to train is that it is easy to overdo it. I was still trying, unsuccessfully, to hang with Andrew's schedule, who was thriving on his strict regimen of doing 20,000 yards per week swimming, 300 miles per week cycling, and 50 miles per week running.

I had decided to remain at home in Woodland Hills after turning down an offer to move to San Diego for a new, all-expenses paid training camp. During my interview with the camp organizer, he told me that if I didn't come down and train with the big boys, I would never amount to anything in the sport. He made eye contact with Andrew, who I had dragged along, uninvited, to the interview, and said, "If you hang around with losers, you'll never reach your potential. You need to surround yourself with the winners and the top coaching we will provide down here in San Diego." I concluded that my setup at home with my parents, training with Andrew and the others, and making some easy money through Johnny G and his personal training setup was preferable to relocating to winner country.

Andrew caught fire at the beginning of the triathlon season and won eight of his first nine triathlons. It was pretty weird to ascend into prominence over the winter, with Andrew the "loser" remaining in obscurity, and then suddenly watch Andrew become overwhelmed with attention after his just as dramatic entrance into the limelight.

We enjoyed some recognition as training partners who had both arrived unexpectedly onto the scene, isolated from all of our professional competition training in Los Angeles.

Andrew credited me, and my sudden success the previous winter, for giving him the inspiration and belief that he could do it too—particularly since he was burying me in training! He confided that his fire was further stoked by the San Diego "loser" interview, along with an innocent comment a friend of mine made to him after my victory, and his 14th place finish, in the January Desert Princess event. My friend said to Andrew, "Great race Andrew, you were only 13 minutes behind Brad!" Little did the friend (Andrew couldn't remember which friend, possible suspects included my future wife Tracy) know of our many close battles in previous races, or of his domination in training.

After my mediocre results in the beginning of the 1987 season, I got my act together and started putting in some good performances. It was Andrew's turn to inspire me as it was he who was the sport's new star; and this helped my motivation and competitive instinct. We tied for a win at the second Bonelli Park race, then Andrew and I finished 1-2, respectively, in the series final, both of us smashing Molina's Bonelli Park course record. This would have been impossible to conceive of the previous year, when I was 14th in the Bonelli series final, seven minutes behind and in awe of the course record time of Molina. It was great to look back and see how far we had both come in one year. We were extremely focused and dedicated to our training and racing. The success of either of us bred more success.

I was racing and training like crazy, gleefully returning to races where I had been blown out one year earlier to achieve different results: third at the Orange County Performing Arts Center triathlon, and first at the San Diego International triathlon, beating Tinley "in his own backyard," as the newspaper story said.

Another memorable week-long trip to Florida was taken, with

my travel companion this time being George Hoover. I had met George on some of my frequent excursions to San Diego to visit Tracy and train at the triathlon mecca of San Diego's north county area. We agreed to take the trip to Florida together for the USTS race in Miami on May 3rd, followed by the Gulf Coast half-Ironman across the state in Panama City Beach on May 9th.

George has a unique perspective on the sport, and life, having enjoyed the lavish excess of JDavid in its heyday (he was the son of J. David Dominelli's girlfriend Nancy Hoover, and was largely responsible for inspiring JDavid's foray into triathlon), and then suffering personally and financially when the firm collapsed. He is a very friendly and fun-loving person, with none of the arrogance that someone in his position might have exuded. He was coming off a breakthrough year in 1986, having finished fifth at the national championships in Hilton Head, South Carolina, and then a tremendous third in Nice, France, the race that I fell apart in.

Although George is laid back and friendly with nearly everyone he meets, people can also get under his skin if they catch him in the right mood. A hilarious example of this occurred at the registration for the Panama City race when he marched right up to the race director and with not so much as a hello announced, "I'm George Hoover." He obviously expected the guy to drop everything and cater to this noted guest of the race. The race director said, "Well hi George Hoover, nice to meet you. I'm Ken Cole, the race director." George was a bit perturbed at his lack of recognition. "Uh, you don't *know* who I am? I'm *George Hoover*, third in Nice." It appeared George had met his match as Ken replied, "Do you know who *I* am?" "No, why should I?" "Well, I've written a book, I'll bet you didn't know that..."

The two had their standoff for a couple of minutes, and when the smoke cleared, I was amazed to see that they had become friends! George even received an autographed copy of the guy's book in the mail when he returned home after the race. I placed fourth, George seventh, and we departed Panama City after the race to drive to Jacksonville, stay overnight, and catch a 7 AM flight home to California the next day.

We were pretty trashed from the difficult half-Ironman, followed by the long drive and then the early morning wake up call, but we groggily made our way in predawn darkness to the airport, dropped the rental car off, and checked in for our flight. As we were waiting at the gate to board the plane, I remembered we had forgotten to fill the rental car with gas, and with plenty of time I ran out of the airport, giving George all of my carry on luggage, to fill it up at a nearby gas station.

I returned to the gate with five minutes to spare, calmly walked up and gave the agent my ticket, and noticed that the plane had pulled out of the gate. I was confused since it was five until seven and asked him what was going on. He replied, "Yep, that flight's left early or on time 21 days in a row." I couldn't believe my ears—a plane actually leaving early? Unheard of! Arguing futilely with this dimwit gate agent, I began to realize the desperation of the situation, and in my exhausted physical state at that ungodly hour, I started to lose it. "No, no! Planes don't leave *early!* You can't leave *early!* I'm on that plane, and it leaves at 7 AM. Bring it back!" "Sorry, can't do that, it's left the gate." "What about my boarding pass? And my friend George? You must have known I was a passenger. Didn't my friend tell you I was coming back?"

I wasn't getting anywhere with this gate agent, but I was in a panic and refused to give up. I sprinted from the gate area to the outside of the terminal, intent on stopping the plane. I noticed an open gate for service vehicles leading to the tarmac, so I ran through it and onto the tarmac. There it was—*my* airplane slowly taxiing out to the runway. I ran out to right below the cockpit window and started yelling and screaming, "I'm on that plane (waving my ticket), bring it back! You can't leave *early."* The plane stopped as the copilot noticed me out his window, and then the other pilot leaned over to look at me too. They seemed very surprised and didn't know what to do; it looked like I had a chance!

Just then I looked behind me and saw a couple of burly redneck airport cops speeding towards me in a golf cart. They grabbed me and threw me into the cart, and my efforts to stop the plane were concluded. As we were driving away, I noticed George laughing and waving to me out of his window.

The cops took me into a little interrogation room and detained me for a couple of hours. A few of the identical looking, pot-bellied-mirror-glasses-alligator-swamp-backwoods-redneck-hillbilly cops took turns asking me the same questions, perhaps as a method to see if I would "crack" and spill the beans about the big terrorist hijacking ring I was a part of. "Do y'all real-ahz that ya committed uh Feh-der-ul ah-fence boy?" "No, sir!" "Have ya a-yeah-ver bee-yin envolved enn enneh tair-wrist ayack-tivity boy?" "No, sir, sorry for the problem sir." (I was just trying to get on my plane that left early from your lousy airport.)

The strong results I had in 1987 were interspersed by several DNFs or very poor finishes as I would regularly become exhausted from the racing and the attempts to maintain my mileage in training. The low point of the year came in Bermuda on August 16th. It was a brand new, high profile event with a $100,000 purse, the richest ever for a short distance race. Nearly every top male and female triathlete in the world was there. I had been pretty burnt out all summer, often sleeping until 11 AM, wishing I could sleep more. My workouts were getting slower and slower, but training by myself at my summer training base of Santa Barbara, I was still deluded into thinking that I could pull off a big race.

Andrew and I had a rough trip; a hurricane had hit the island before we arrived, messing up all of the scheduled flights, and we didn't arrive until the middle of the night on the day before the race. I was flat right from the beginning, had a terrible swim, and was soon completely out of contention, lingering at the back of the pack on the bike. By the time I finished the bike, I was so disinterested and discouraged that I just jogged through the run, finishing 31st in the deep field.

Hours after the race, to add insult to injury, ten guys were disqualified for drafting violations in a couple of huge packs that formed on the narrow roads on the island. What this meant was that if I had simply bothered to produce a decent effort on the run, I would have finished in the revised top 20 and taken home an easy $1,000. I was devastated by the whole experience and flew off the island to New York practically shaking from the shock and disappointment over what had transpired.

When things are going well with racing, the travel aspect of the career is enjoyable and relaxing. I use the travel time to catch up on reading, write letters, postcards, or training articles, sleep, listen to music on the Walkman, or converse with the people I meet during my journey. With all this to do, time flies even on long trips, and aggravation and boredom are rare. After a good race, I'm wired and feeling euphoric, a five-hour flight feels like one, a flight delay means more time to read my book, etc. The same is true for traveling to a race. I'm excited about the race and eager to travel to the city, check out the sights, and mingle with my peers for the weekend. I don't even mind lugging around my bike case, the biggest pain of all in triathlon.

When a race goes poorly, travel can be a real hassle. I'm tired, cranky, and just want to be home. The bike case feels like it weighs a thousand pounds, and every minor travel hassle seems to throw me for a loop. You might say my trip home from Bermuda sucked. When Andrew and I got to New York, we found out our LA flight was overbooked and we were probably going to be bumped off. We also found out that we had just missed a plane to LA with some empty seats while we were killing time in the snack bar. We were able to switch flights and boarded our alternate plane, only to be treated to a three hour mechanical delay, all of which was spent on the plane with continuing announcements of "about another 20 minutes to a half-hour and we should be on our way." When we arrived in LA in the middle of the night (again), I was physically and emotionally spent. The baggage, of course, was delayed after we arrived. I had half a mind to just leave my bike at the airport and never race again.

16

EIGHT HOURS AND A STOP SIGN

What I needed was a break from my excessive training and racing schedule, so Tracy and I took a driving vacation to Northern California. Soon I was feeling refreshed and ready to train again, particularly when I could explore the new surroundings during our trip. We ended up at Lake Tahoe, in the Sierra Nevada mountains on the border of California and Nevada, where Andrew was vacationing at his family home.

Andrew suggested that we enter the ultra-distance World's Toughest triathlon, slated for a week after we arrived—on a lark—to get in a long, hard workout. It was a brutal course, and I had no desire to finish the whole thing as I had races scheduled for September, and recovering from ultra-distance races takes quite a while. The course featured a two-mile swim in the chilly waters of Lake Tahoe, a 100-mile bike ride over three mountain passes, and finished with a very hilly 18.6-mile trail run, all at an altitude of 6,000 feet or more above sea level. Andrew and I agreed to do the swim and bike segments then drop out before the brutal trail run, saving our legs and getting in an excellent workout to prepare for the upcoming shorter races on the circuit.

Tracy had scheduled a job interview in LA and needed to return home before the race weekend, so we arranged for her to fly home from nearby Reno, Nevada, while I would drive home after the race. Her flight was the day before the race, so I figured I would spin my legs by riding from Tahoe down to Carson City, Nevada, meet Tracy, and drive her on to the Reno airport. Carson City and Reno are located in the Nevada desert below the mountains surrounding Lake Tahoe, so the ride would be a mostly downhill 40-miler, nothing too strenuous to interfere with the big effort the following day.

I reached Carson City and waited and waited with no sign of Tracy. I called Andrew from a pay phone and he informed me she had left hours before—I had missed her somehow. I was forced to turn around and climb some 3,000 feet over Spooner summit and back to South Lake Tahoe. Five hours and 80 miles later, I was back from my little pre-race spin, soon followed by Tracy, who was forced to return with the car and miss her flight.

The next day my legs felt great on the first two major mountain passes of the ride. I found myself with a huge lead when early leader Andrew flatted and withdrew from the race. I arrived at the bike to run transition area 15 minutes ahead of the next rider and had no choice but to scrap my plans to retire early and carry on. It is not too often that one finds themselves with a 15-minute lead in a race, and to drop out would have been disgraceful. Besides, an unexpected win would certainly be worth the sacrifice of missing a few upcoming races while recovering. I felt great the entire run, bantering with the TV cameramen covering the race, and maintained my 15 minute lead crossing the line. It was a great way to bounce back from a mostly disappointing summer.

After mingling at the finish line for a while, we went home to Andrew's where I cleaned up and went down for a nap before our planned celebration that evening. Later, Andrew woke me from my nap to accept a phone call. Hmm. The media calling? No, it was the race director. Sorry to break the news that I had been disqualified from the race! My infraction was that I failed to stop for a stop sign on the bike ride. As the course was not closed to traffic, riders were obliged to obey all traffic laws during the race. There were a couple of stop signs in the mountains at highway junctions, necessitating a foot down stop by all athletes. I remember having a police motorcycle escort through most of the ride, who blared his siren into each intersection, announcing the arrival of the front of the race and halting traffic so I could come through. Thus, I felt no need to stop at the intersections.

Our night of celebration was postponed by a return to the finish area for a long meeting and debate with the race organizers. I was hoping perhaps they could declare a time penalty as opposed to an outright disqualification for an infraction saving a few seconds in an eight hour race, but the decision stood.

It was pretty upsetting, and my reaction was to take out my frustrations on my body and the road. Instead of resting after the race, I plunged into heavy training, intent on racing the upcoming races that I assumed I would miss. My fury fueled me for a couple weeks, but soon I was in a deep hole of exhaustion.

My first trip to the Hawaii Ironman was a month and a half later, and I was still exhausted from the ordeal and the silly punishment I had inflicted on myself. I made it through 80 miles of the bike ride, then got hot and tired and struggled in, getting passed by dozens. I halfheartedly jogged the first few miles of the run until I reached my condo at the five-mile mark. My family was there cheering for me, and to their surprise, I stopped, chatted with them for a while, and then announced I was going into the condo to take a shower and eat lunch.

17

A TEAM SPORT?

I had established myself as one of the top young racers on the circuit after my season, albeit inconsistent, in 1987. Besides my stock portfolio featuring one percent of the fast-growing clothing company Edgewear, I had a few sponsorship deals that brought in a little extra bonus money for good race results. Before the 1988 season, I was offered a spot on a new, big budget triathlon team sponsored by Pioneer Electronics, and organized by an acquaintance of mine from the LA triathlon scene, Scott Zagarino. Andrew was offered a position as well, and our deals were secured when Scott elected to have Edgewear, whom we were obligated to "for life," outfit the team. We signed on the dotted line for compensation of $4,000 in travel expense reimbursement.

The new Pioneer team would feature some of the biggest names in the sport, like top females Sylviane and Patricia Puntous from Canada and American Colleen Cannon. It was a privilege, at least initially, to be a part of it. Over the winter we had a team meeting, with all the members flown into LA from their respective cities, featuring a lavish banquet where the big-time public relations firm hired to promote the team gave a slick presentation on how important we were to Pioneer. Then we had an all-day poster shoot, complete with makeup artists and hair stylists fussing with us in between shots. Several of the athletes on the team who were based in LA were beneficiaries of a team coach and massage therapist, who we could meet with once a week for guided workouts and massage sessions.

I had moved from my parents house in Woodland Hills to Malibu with Tracy where we lived right on the beach on the PCH. I would regularly ride from my new home back to the Valley to train with the gang, which had now dwindled to just Andrew, pro duathlete Marc DeLeon, and a young pro triathlete named Eric Cech. Soon I had my former nemesis Topanga Canyon wired from the frequent commute.

Andrew and I were attempting to follow a strict training schedule laid out for us by Dave Scott, who had won his sixth Ironman the previous year. We spoke with him at an awards banquet in January of 1988, and he invited us to his Northern California home in Davis, outside of Sacramento, to discuss our training with him. When Andrew called to make arrangements, Dave offered us two hours of his time, an hour at night and an hour the next morning. We drove all day to Davis and met him in the early evening at his office, talking for a while, then went over to the University of California, Davis to run with a group of athletes he was coaching. Dave didn't feel like running and just hung out while we ran. We couldn't believe it—here was the Ironman champ and he didn't even want to train!

After the next morning's meeting, we had our schedules set and raced home, psyched to put them into effect. We were absolutely amazed at Dave's training philosophy as he was really down on high mileage training and urged us to emphasize specific, race-pace workouts, eliminating much of the long, slow stuff that was our staple for so long. Dave's image was of a man who trained all day in solitude in the heat and wind of Davis and the surrounding farmlands, and thus our surprise at his apparent change of heart. He confided to us that he used to literally train all day in his early years, but got sick of it and decided that there had to be a better way. He told us that before his great Ironman victory over Mark Allen in 1987, his longest training run was only 18 miles and longest ride under 100 miles.

If it worked for Dave, surely it could work for me, and I implemented the new training plan immediately. I had a tough time with all the intensity and was only able to meet a fraction of the suggested weekly plan. I still felt like I was getting fast, and was primed for a big result at the Desert Princess championships on February 20th, 1988. I finished fifth in the Championships, not bad, but lacking any of the magic that I'd had the previous winter. I even found out what the Dirt

Road from Hell was all about as I died on the second run and was passed by Paul Huddle.

After the race, I questioned my new schedule and whether the low mileage I was putting in had sapped my strength and endurance. I sought out Mark Allen and Kenny Souza in the finish area to discuss training. Kenny turned in another incredible victory, destroying his old course record and finishing three and a half minutes ahead of runner-up Scott Tinley while Allen lost some 20 minutes due to a wheel problem.

I asked Kenny and Mark about their training programs, and they both echoed the need for long distance, comfortably paced, aerobic base-building training. Allen discussed how this training allows the aerobic system to develop fully, the foundation for success in endurance events. He said too much fast-paced, intense training is stressful to the body and drains the adrenal glands, causing the body to become fatigued regularly and produce poor performances, overtraining and injuries. With a strong aerobic foundation, the body is able to handle the occasional stress of race pace workouts and thrive off of them.

Souza was less eloquent about his training philosophy but nevertheless like-minded. "Long rides, man, long rides. That's what got me here, there's no substitute."

I certainly didn't interpret each athlete's training philosophy perfectly, but it seemed like a direct contradiction in methods among the top athletes. Since I was having such trouble following my program anyway, and disappointed with my Desert Princess race, I junked the Dave Scott program and started hitting the roads and trails, putting in increasingly more training hours for the next six weeks.

Two of the biggest races in the history of the sport were fast approaching: a half-Ironman in St. Croix, Virgin Islands, followed by a long-distance race in Queensland, Australia. Each new race promised an excess of $100,000 in prize money. I was training out of my mind and getting increasingly confident that I would be able to challenge anyone at these races. Then, about two weeks before St. Croix, my body totally crashed and I suddenly had no energy to do even a fraction of my previous workload.

I would suffer these crashes repeatedly throughout my career, always coming unexpectedly on the heels of superhuman periods of training. This phenomenon, I believe, is related to the function of the body's adrenal glands. As more and more stress is piled on in the form of training, or anything in life, the body tries mightily to keep up, and the stress response hormones flow freely to enable all of the body's systems to function at a high level.

If the stress is unrelenting, eventually the effect is exhausted and the hormone output falls to much lower than normal while the body recovers from the overload. Many of the common symptoms of overtraining are the result of diminished function of the adrenal glands, such as: joint pain in the knees and lower back, poor sleeping and digestion, cravings for sugar, moodiness and irritability, poor concentration, and an apathetic attitude towards training.

Flying to a race while knowing deep down that you are cooked is no fun. I try to put on my game face, but it always disappears when the gun goes off and the pain begins. I finished a pathetic 14th in St. Croix, totally crushed because I knew that I was in tremendous shape and had just overdone my preparations to the point of being exhausted when I stepped to the starting line.

The next race, World Cup Australia, was even worse than St. Croix. It was held in Surfers Paradise, Queensland, on Australia's Gold Coast resort area. It was an ultra-distance race (1.8-mile swim, 80-mile bike, 20-mile run) and the purse was the largest in the history of the sport, $160,000. It was a golden opportunity for the handful of Americans who traveled to the race. I had struggled with my training since St. Croix, but was still optimistic that I could pull off a great result and cash in big time. I had nothing again and bonked about 60 miles into the bike ride. I dropped out after the bike and watched Mark Allen beat Scott Tinley and take home $30,000.

Every American who showed up and crossed the finish line took home a huge loot. I remember Ray Browning and Kenny Souza, whom I shared a condo with, coming home from the awards ceremony ecstatic after totalling up their take of the prize purse and the generous bonuses for top split times to be around $10,000 each. I flew home dejected, realizing I had squandered an extremely golden opportunity.

It seemed like someone or something was testing my will in 1988, and I encountered more bad luck and poor performances as the season continued. While racing in second place behind eventual winner Andrew in Orange County, my pedal suddenly broke off my bike, ending my race. I finally got a win at the Huntington Beach triathlon in June, a small relief from a confidence crushing early season. The high note didn't last long as I totally bombed out the next week at another big race, the $80,000 Heritage International triathlon in Provo, Utah. The whole Pioneer team attended the race together, which only added to the disappointment of my 17th place.

I was having a difficult time conforming to be a member of a team. The camaraderie on the Pioneer team was great, but we pros already had that, plus we could pick and choose who we wanted to hang out with. I remember leaving to the airport one morning the day after a race. I was running late, and a female Pioneer team member was having an absolute fit waiting for me in the team rental car. "I'm gonna miss my flight! Oh God, Oh God, I'm gonna miss my flight" I thought to myself, *Am I back at Peat Marwick with the ABs? Why am I traveling with this person anyway, just because we're teammates?*

I prefer to be independent and responsible for my own success or failure. In the sports leagues I participated in as a youth, it always annoyed me when other athletes didn't take the game as seriously as I did. I would even be disappointed if they tried their best but didn't come through, a poor sport I guess, although I never verbalized my disappointment.

I was attracted to activities like golf and running, individual sports where the athlete lives and dies by his or her own actions. But even these sports are organized in a team manner for scholastic competition, so I still had problems. This was evident from my experiences as a runner on the UCSB teams. I suffered more than thrived as a result of my teammates and coach. Left to my own devices, I undoubtedly would have done better than the pathetic results I achieved in college.

When I was finally free from the shackles of people exerting influence over my athletic career, I was able to find my best success. I know there is a trade-off, that one can never reach their full potential without competition from others, but it seemed like whenever I crossed that line and sought to include myself in a group, I took a step backward. Beginning my career in triathlon, I needed to become proficient in swimming and biking, so I joined the UCSB cycling team. It was almost entirely a negative experience. All I learned was that I hated the sport of cycling! Then I sought out a swim team as everyone urges a novice swimmer to do if they want to improve. What happened? An aloof, poorly communicating coach destroyed the stroke and confidence of a fairly talented swimmer, a huge step backward.

What I like most is when a group of one or more individuals can fit smoothly into my routine. Training with Andrew early in our careers was successful as we were both focused on the same thing and knew our training habits. Similarly, my sojourns to San Diego to visit Tracy and train in the triathlon mecca were also effective. I would pop down for a couple of days, usually Tuesday and Wednesday, when the hardest group workouts of the week took place, the famed Tuesday run, a 12-mile fast paced trail run, and then the Wednesday ride, a fast and furious 80-miler along the coast in a huge, aggressive pack. By Wednesday afternoon, I'd always be wasted. Time to head home and rest while the locals would often carry on with group overtraining and burn themselves out.

One agreement I always try to establish with a training partner is that it is OK to flake on a workout for any reason. This way, feelings of obligation or guilt trips will not make someone go against their instincts and train simply because they agreed to and don't want to upset their workout partners. I don't mind being considered a flake, capable of disappearing from workout obligations at any time without warning. The alternative of being Mr. Reliable might be honorable, but I believe that not obeying your instincts and acting in your own best interests about training, shows up in race results.

It has been difficult to find these perfect fits into the personal routines I establish over time, particularly with the more regimented sport of swimming. One group I had great success with was the CLASS Aquatics age-group team located in Calabasas. Unfortunately, I was only able to enjoy the situation for about a year before I moved to Northern California. The team was coached by Bud McAllister, an age-group coach of several national champions, including Janet Evans during her preparations for her three golds at the 1988 Olympics. Many of the members of the CLASS team were competitive nationally, so

Andrew and I were among the slowest swimmers in the pool full of kids.

The CLASS workouts were so long and hard that we had to sneak out early, tail between our legs, after swimming 5,000 yards, a huge total for a triathlete. I didn't have to worry about a spotty attendance record because the workouts were so hard I would always need at least a day to recover afterwards.

The best part about Bud's workouts was his no nonsense approach. Instead of messing around with endless stroke technique drills, or using aids like pull buoys, swim paddles, and fins, Bud believes in swimming long and fast to get the best results. Workouts began with a 15 minute warm-up, then we'd head into a long, brutal freestyle set. 30 to 40 minutes later we'd get to stop and catch our breath. With everyone in the pool working hard, resting little, and concentrating on the specifics of the swim set, the workouts flew by, with little mental effort expended.

Although he was coaching teenagers, it was a highly motivated group. All of the swimmers were fully aware of the price they needed to pay for success. Rather than being a disciplinarian, Bud dealt with the kids in a mature manner, always with the implication that they were not forced to swim, that they chose to. Bud told me that parents would sometimes complain about the arduous workout schedule that had the kids swimming from 5:30 to 7 each morning before school, followed by a harder workout after school from 4 to 6:30. Bud always explained to them that the schedule would not change—for that's what they needed to prepare for national competition—but that kids were always welcome to drop down to a lower group and swim less.

18

HEROES ARE BORN OUT OF SUFFERING

I've had some epic low points in my career, but few rival the feeling I had after the World Cup Australia race in 1988. Seeing Kenny Souza and Ray Browning come back to our condo, ecstatic about the ten grand they would each take home, brought up a harsh realization for me. In less than a year's time, I had placed myself at the starting line of four of the biggest races in the sport: 1987 Bermuda, 1987 Ironman, 1988 St. Croix, and 1988 World Cup Australia, traveling all over the world to do so, and taken home a grand total of zero dollars in prize money.

Perhaps the worst mistake of all was failing to place myself on the starting line of another race when I absolutely should have. That race was in Perth, Australia on January 18th, 1987, one week after the race of my life in Palm Springs. Featuring a $100,000 purse, it was the World Sprint Championships. The Big Four—Allen, Molina, Scott, and Tinley—were all enticed to attend, no doubt by large appearance fees as each of them were admittedly out of shape due to the time of year.

It was a perfect opportunity for me as I was one of the few pros in the world in top shape that January, perhaps joined by a few contenders from down under in the midst of their summer racing season. Molina told me after the Desert Princess race that I should definitely go to Perth the next weekend. I was intrigued and checked into a flight, which ran $1,500, all of my first place prize money from Palm Springs plus $500, a huge risk. I was apprehensive about the long flight to the West coast of Australia, and the eight hour time change (with memories of my zombie week in Nice), so I chickened out.

Bad, bad decision. A young pro from New Zealand named Richard Wells blew everyone away for the $16,000 first prize and instant recognition around the world for being the first man ever to knock off all of the Big Four in a single race. They were perhaps never more ripe for picking than that day in January of 1987. Molina, who I had beaten by eight minutes the week before, caught a cold before the race and still finished ninth, picking up a few grand for his meek effort. It didn't take a genius to figure out that my fitness level predicted a very high finish had I just gone to the race. Julie Brening, the female winner of the Desert Princess race, took the risk, flew to the race, and came home with a second place and $10,000.

My head spun when I heard the results. I realized that I didn't believe in myself enough to take a risk and go to a race when I was in the shape of my life. I vowed that I would never be intimidated by traveling or competition again. If I wanted to play it safe, I could go back to the accounting firm.

Perhaps this vow is what got me to a few starting lines that I shouldn't have been at. Being in an unstructured, individual sport does present frequent dilemmas with regards to race selection, deciding how, when, where, and with whom to train, and also what to decide on business matters like negotiating with sponsors. The poor decisions I have made and the resulting misfortunes have been the greatest source of frustration in my career. I can handle getting my butt kicked in a race and quickly move on, but if I skip a great opportunity like Perth, show up poorly prepared at a race due to mistakes I made in training, or blow through a stop sign and get disqualified, it eats at me for a long time.

I feel that enduring my setbacks and realizing that no one can take the blame for them has made me stronger. In order to continue to survive in this career, I can't let my misfortunes break me. I have to learn from them and move on. These lessons are more significant and long lasting than those I learn from winning. When I win, everything is easy—I am made of blue sky, and golden light, and will feel this way forever—just like the guy in the perfume commercial. When I lose a race, blow a business decision, or fall weakness to compulsion and screw up my training, I have to look in the mirror and ask those hard questions: Why did I do that when I knew it was stupid? Am I afraid of success? Do I lack the confidence deep down to go after what I want? Am I self-sabotaging my career?

Sometimes the answers are not pretty, but the only way one grows is to confront the truth and decide to do something about it. If I had given up on triathlon and gone back to accounting or whatever, it might have been easier in many ways, but I would have missed out on many things and regretted it forever. I think many people have done this in their lives, given up on something or not believed in themselves, and are filled with regret from it. This is one of my biggest fears; the clock is always ticking, and every day of not being true to myself and my dreams is a day wasted. This doesn't mean I advocate closing up shop and heading out West to strike gold. It means that I believe that whatever you do in life, it is important to enjoy it and to do your best. The rewards of everything we do have to come from within, so if you enjoy what you do and do your best, that is the highest success you can ever achieve.

This is much easier said than done. When I fall flat on my face trying, it is still a bummer. To experience the difference between doing something for enjoyment and with pure motives, and doing something out of compulsion, for approval of others, or any of the other wrong reasons, helps to keep life and one's priorities in the proper perspective. This is one way I find value in struggle and setbacks, for these occasions force me to look at the true reasons why I do something much more than successful occasions. When successful, the external, superficial stimuli—money, adulation from others, recognition—dominate the picture and the true motives don't need to be addressed. The ego grows so big that there is no room for them!

Conversely, when times are hard, I ask myself if I really love what I'm doing and if it's for the right reasons. After World's Toughest, a big part of me was frustrated with the DQ, but another part of me, insignificant in the immediate aftermath yet still in my awareness, knew that nothing could take away from what I had accomplished during the eight hours on the course; I got to enjoy the cheers of the crowd, break the tape, and share the day with my friends.

When I abused myself in training after the race, the compulsive, superficial part of me had won out as I was focused on the DQ, the loss of income, and the obsession to return to the race course and redeem myself. Had the other side of me won out, I would have respected the performance I turned in, regardless of the DQ, and given my body the rest it needed afterwards. I would have been satisfied that I had reached my ultimate goal of doing my best. Factors I have no control over, like whether I finish in first place or get DQed, would be of minor concern. Ideally they are not my true motives for doing the sport.

Years later, I look back with fond memories of my race in Lake Tahoe, for I grew tremendously as an athlete from the ordeal, and with time healing any wounds, only the positive memories remain. When striving to live by the philosophy of doing my best and remain pure in my motives, I am able to treat setbacks as a test to reaffirm that my attitude is in the right place.

I have dropped out of many races. Usually the only thing to do is to hang around and watch the winners come in. When in this situation, I always ask myself what I am feeling at the time. Sometimes I feel jealousy or envy towards the winners, an indication that I am way out of balance and need an attitude adjustment. Usually I am able to feel happiness for the winners, for I know how hard they worked and how deserving they are of their success. When my head is in the right place, I can experience the full weight of my disappointment from dropping out of the race, then immediately let it go and watch the other athletes perform and enjoy their success.

It is well known that the ability to live in the present is crucial to a happy and satisfying life. Athletics is a great vehicle for striving to live in the present, for success is graphically dependent on it. When Michael Jordan goes to the free-throw line late in a championship game, his mind has to be in the present moment, focused on the task, not on the bad shot he took last time down the court or a bad call by the referee. The same is true for Jack Nicklaus standing over a crucial putt, Andre Agassi serving in the fifth set, Joe Montana on a fourth quarter touchdown drive, or a triathlete trying to deal with pain in a race.

When an athlete carries around emotional baggage, like regrets or anger from the past, or fear and uncertainty about the future, performance will always suffer. It's a challenge to stay in the present, but in sports the pitfalls of the mind wandering are constant and powerful. It is a far more difficult challenge to live in the present in everyday life as we easily can fall into habits and routines of dealing with ourselves and others that can become negative and debilitating.

An example is the emotional baggage people carry with them from childhood throughout their adult life. People who felt victimized or neglected in some way early in life let these experiences shape and define their personality for years afterwards, negatively affecting their lives and relations with others. In a pure and straightforward arena like athletics, negative thoughts and behavior—such as a lack of confidence or fear of success—are shoved right in your face. No matter what level or sport you compete at, you are laying it on the line, risking and exposing yourself for all to see. You receive instant, unassailable feedback in the form of results, where there is little chance for misinterpretation or rationalization.

Most everyone has had the experience of choking in an athletic endeavor. This occurs when we don't perform up to our capabilities when the importance of the contest is high. We may be able to hit our golf drives long and straight on the driving range, then when we step up to the first tee with everyone watching and the score counting, we freeze up and hit it into the trees.

The specific reasons for choking may be varied as we like to manufacture excuses and rationalize about our failures. But there is a common thread to all these occasions, no matter what the sport or whether it's a neighborhood game or the Super Bowl, and that is the mind has interfered with and hindered the body's performance by increasing nervous tension. The muscles and nerves need to be relaxed for optimum performance and hand-eye coordination. Usually this tension is a result of fearful thoughts, about whether we will be able to perform how we want or expect to, about the uncertainty of the outcome, or a fear of repeating past failures—all thought patterns that result from not remaining in the present moment.

Many champions have spoken of things happening automatically, without even trying, during top performances. They don't even feel the pain involved and certainly not the pressure. Some of Joe Montana's San Francisco 49er teammates said after their Super Bowl victory in 1989 over the Cincinnati Bengals that they sensed in the huddle in the fourth quarter that Joe was absolutely certain he would lead the team to a score and the victory. There was a complete lack of tension, no uncertainty about the outcome or fear of failure; Joe knew they would score. When an athlete can reach this state of consciousness, success is virtually assured.

19

LATE 88, THINGS GOING GREAT

Just as it did after Bermuda in 1987, a mid-season vacation and break from training brought me out of my slump in 1988. After my glorious 17th place in Provo, I was exhausted, frustrated and depressed about my poor results and bad luck. I needed a break, so Tracy and I shoved off from Provo, Utah after the race and toured the national parks in the area, visiting Bryce Canyon and Zion in Utah, then taking a camping trip in the Grand Canyon. When I returned home, I felt completely refreshed and my workouts were soon better than ever.

I returned to the circuit for a couple races in Canada, highlighted by a sixth place at the World Championships in Kelowna, British Columbia. It was an intense race—a huge pack finished the bike together, all chasing after Mike Pigg, who had a lead of about one minute, 40 seconds beginning the run. The pack got smaller and smaller as people dropped off the pace during the run. Mark Allen and Stephen Foster of Australia almost caught Pigg in the homestretch, but he held them off for a gallant victory. I was ecstatic to be able to mix it up with the big boys again, and was eagerly looking forward to upcoming races.

One memorable weekend came in September when I traveled to Cleveland for the National City triathlon. Midway through the bike leg, I was riding with Canadian Nick Taylor and Lance Armstrong, a 16-year-old pro from Texas who became the world cycling champion in 1993. We were battling for second place, behind leader Rip Esselstyn of Texas, when I looked back and noticed that we were far ahead of the rest of the field. Comfortable that I could outrun Rip, Nick and Lance, I was suddenly overcome with this feeling that I would definitely win the race. Just when the feeling hit me, my pedal broke off my bike, just as it had in Orange County.

After the Orange County incident I had called up my pedal sponsor and chewed him out, informing him of how much money I likely had lost because of his cheap ass pedals. He was very apologetic and sent me a brand new pair, promising it would never happen again. But there I was, stuck out in the Cleveland suburbs on a bike with one pedal. I began slowly pedaling with one leg back to downtown Cleveland and found my way onto the run course to see how the race was progressing. I saw Andrew, who would end up sixth, and he noticed that my pedal had broken again. He told me—while running—that there was a pro race in Sacramento, California, scheduled for the next day. He said he would go, so I one-legged it to the nearest phone booth and tried to make reservations to fly back to Sacramento instead of Los Angeles.

The airlines would not authorize us to change our tickets, but when we arrived at the Cleveland airport, we devised a scheme to get to Sacramento as painless as possible. One of my hobbies (out of necessity as a starving pro athlete) is to try to beat the airlines at their silly game of rules and restrictions when flying with them. As far as getting from point A to point B, where there's a will, there's almost always a way, and it's amazing what the airlines will do to get you out of their hair if you are persistent enough. If I had been passive every time a possible glitch in my travel plans came up, I'd have a lot more days logged on the road and many more hours spent idling in airports.

When Andrew and I arrived at the Cleveland airport and were told again unequivocally that we had to return to LA with our tickets, we said thank you and walked to the Sacramento gate, lined up with the passengers and boarded the plane. ("Oh, this is going to *Sacramento....* Gosh! My mistake. Oh well, whatever, it's still California.") Upon arrival at the race headquarters in Sacramento, we had to beg the race director Sally Edwards to let us do the race. She gave us a little lecture about being responsible professionals and informing races of our plans in advance, instead of crashing them last minute. I tried to explain that I hadn't planned to break my pedal, but mostly thanked her for letting me enter. With Andrew loaning me a spare pair of pedals, everything was set to go for weekend race #2.

The stress of the day had me so wired I couldn't sleep, and I tossed and turned all night, intent on redeeming myself and salvaging the weekend.

I felt great in the race and earned a comfortable victory worth $2,000, definitely salvaging the weekend.

Next was a return to Nice for the third time to try and improve on my 20th place from 1987. Things had improved for Andrew and I each year, from the anonymous rookies dragging their luggage through town in 1986, to being provided a complementary room in a hotel with all the other athletes in 1987, to being provided a flight and a room for 1988, by virtue of my top 20 finish the previous year.

My training had gone great as we again put in the requisite specific training rides up Piuma road in the Santa Monica mountains to prepare for the Alps. I finished the bike with Scott Tinley in sixth and seventh, and had a solid run to finish in sixth place. I now had a sixth in the World Long Distance Championships to go with my sixth at the World Sprint Championships in Kelowna, by far my best results in big time races. It was the first time since my Desert Princess victories in the winter of 1986-87 that I felt like I was performing up to my capabilities and potential. I was satisfied with the direction my career was going in and looking forward to the future.

There was one major race left on the 1988 schedule, the second annual Bermuda triathlon in late October. Again a $100,000 purse was featured and a generous airline sponsor allowed the race director, Patrick O'Riordan, to offer any pro of note a free airfare and luxury accommodations in the Southampton Princess. Any pro of note except Brad Kearns or Andrew MacNaughton. For some reason, all of our overtures to the race organizers were ignored; we could not receive an invitation, even as we knew of many lesser athletes receiving the whole travel package. We found out later that some 50 tickets were given out, including some to girl/boy friends accompanying pro racers.

We were totally perplexed as to why we were denied, and with a little digging, we discovered that the race director had a low opinion of us for an unspecified reason, and refused to invite us due to our bad reputation. Neither of us had much contact with him the previous year for him to form an opinion of us; we hadn't been among those disqualified for drafting, so we hadn't the foggiest idea what his problem with us was. We had to shell out $600 to fly there and then mooch some floor space off our teammate George Hoover at the Southampton Princess. At the pro meeting before the race, the NBC film crew read a list of names of about 40 athletes who they requested a brief taped interview with, on the odd chance that they would become a factor in the race. Andrew and I looked around the room and noticed that we were practically the only ones whose names weren't called for interviews.

Feeling disturbed by these slights was petty of us (except for the $600 airfares) but it served as sufficient motivation to do some damage on race day. We both had terrible swims in the stormy ocean, but soon we were riding through to the front of a field decimated by crashes on the wet roads. Andrew rode and ran in second place for most of the race, behind Mark Allen, who was having a brilliant race. I towed a growing pack of guys I couldn't shake. A couple of times I got a gap but then took wrong turns on the confusing course, allowing them to catch back up. I flew into one intersection, noticed at the last minute that the course turned left, slammed on my brakes, and skidded across the width of the lane, barely staying upright and on the road to make the turn. Not so lucky behind me was Ken Glah, who, obviously swayed by my indecision, barreled into the intersection and them went down in a heap when he hit his brakes trying too late to negotiate the turn. Sorry, buddy!

I got off the bike with Tinley and some others. The two of us set a furious pace, soon moving into third and fourth behind Mark and Andrew. We caught Andrew at five miles, then Tinley dropped me on the final brutal hill up to the Southampton Princess and the finish line, and I finished third. I was $6,500 richer and swelling with pride that I, along with my seedy cohort Andrew, had shown everybody who had ignored us at the race that they were wrong. Team director Scott was ecstatic for me after the race and begged NBC commentator John Naber to give me a finish line interview, describing me as an uninvited athlete, sleeping on the floor, who had made it to the podium.

I was still pumped after Bermuda, so I extended my season as far as it could go, racing a biathlon in New York City the following week, and then traveling to Israel for a race at the end of November. I was pretty apprehensive about the Israel trip since it seemed so far away and such an unusual place to hold a triathlon. But I still had some Pioneer travel money left over, and remembering my vow after my Perth decision, took the risk and jumped on a plane for the longest trip of my life. It was pretty scary. I flew from Los Angeles on a Wednesday morning, to New York, then Paris, then to Tel Aviv, then transferred to a domestic airport across town for the hour-long flight from Tel Aviv to the resort town of Eilat, on the Red Sea. By the time I arrived at my hotel, it was late Thursday night, 30 hours after I'd left home in LA and ten times zones East. All of that put me into another complete jet-lag induced haze. I couldn't sleep all night, but near dawn fell asleep and woke around 2:30 PM the next day.

I finished third, earning $1,000. I guess I felt a sense of relief with my finish, and the completion of the season, for that afternoon I impulsively parted with my entire prize money, buying Tracy an engagement ring at a jewelry store in Eilat. There were billboards and flyers everywhere announcing Israel as the "jewelry capital of the world," so I figured what the heck.

We got engaged on Christmas of 1988, and I decided to make her work for the ring just as I had. Before arriving at her parents house in Cardiff on a rainy Christmas night, I stopped off at her old high school, went out to the playground, and climbed up the rope climb installed on the blacktop. At the top, some 20 feet in the air, I taped the gift box with the ring to the metal standard holding up the ropes.

Then I went to her house and grabbed her, along with her sister Kerry to witness, telling her she needed to come to the high school to get her Christmas gift. We went out to the playground and I shined a flashlight up through the raindrops at the gift dangling at the top of the rope. She was pretty brave, and with some coaching by Kerry, a former champion gymnast, got to the top, swatted the box to the ground, and then excitedly shot down the rope to the ground, getting a major case of rope burn. I popped the question at the bottom—she had to say yes after all that work!

20

TAKE WHAT YOU CAN GET

The last chapter in the Pioneer debacle was written in the winter of 1988, and I learned some harsh economic realities from the experience. As the 1988 season wound down, Pioneer team started running out of money, and the athletes ended up not getting all of their promised reimbursements. I was personally out for my Bermuda and Israel tickets charged to my credit card while Andrew's situation was far worse. He had covered some team expenses on his personal credit card; a ticket to Europe for another athlete, a condo for the team in Hilton Head, South Carolina as well as some of his own travel expenses. We never got any of the money back, which was a harsh blow and left a bitter taste in our mouths about the whole Pioneer experience.

Pioneer wanted to put the experience of 1988 behind them and were organizing a team for 1989 with a new manager named Jay Mueller. At a lunch meeting with Jay to discuss my possibly joining the 1989 team, I asked for a lot of money, more than I was worth, partly to make up for the frustration of the previous year. To my surprise, he gave me his word on my compensation request; I agreed to sign with the team.

At a follow-up meeting to finalize the deal, where I sent Tracy's father Bern to represent me for legal expertise, Jay completely denied our verbal agreement, and out of the blue offered a much lower salary. Bern was confused since I had briefed him on the previous discussion and the dollar amounts agreed to, and he broke off the meeting at an impasse. Andrew had similar difficulties in his negotiations, and after an unproductive conference call with Jay, Andrew, and myself, we both decided to keep our pride and reject his final offer. The problem was the offer was very generous—a $12,500 annual cash salary, more than triple the previous years' compensation.

Jay apparently realized his early error in assessing our market values, and figured we would accept his generous final offer. We were being completely stubborn and stupid in putting him off as we had nothing remotely close to the Pioneer offer to fall back on. In one of our many discussions on the subject, I realized that I was suffering from an inflated value of myself—perhaps I needed to change my motto from, "I'm bitchin'" to "take what you can get."

During the conference call with Jay, he categorized Andrew and me as members of a large group of "second tier" pros, whose values were interchangeable to sponsors. After hanging up, I was exasperated and told Andrew that the guy was clueless for saying that as I personally ranked myself seventh in the world the previous season, "behind Pigg, Allen, Glah, etc." Andrew had this strange look on his face during my diatribe. When I climbed down off my high horse and stopped talking, he quietly commented, "Funny you say that, because I thought I had a better season than you did."

At first I was annoyed—how could he say such a thing when it was so obvious that I had a better season than he? Upon further reflection, I realized that my ranking system was severely clouded by self-importance, no doubt the same for Andrew's personal assessment of his season. It became apparent how this attitude affected my negotiations with Pioneer. I didn't think I was interchangeable with all those guys, but Pioneer did, so that was my market value. By the time I called Pioneer, with my pride stashed in the rubbish bin, and announced that I would accept their offer, the team had been filled. My principles had cost me 12 grand.

The poor decision ate at me for quite a while, just like Perth. Instead of having positive, optimistic thoughts about the 1989 season, and careful, controlled preparation, I was bitter and vengeful, and it showed in my training program. Every bike ride was a rolling bitch session about the unfairness of the sport, the lies we were told, and the money we were owed. I thought this fury was serving as motivation as I was hammering my brains out preparing for the first two big races of the year, a return to the World Cup Australia, and a month later Nice, France, with its new June date. I was making the same mistake I did in 1988 before St. Croix and Australia, training like a madman. I got into unbelievable shape, and was finally able to put in some serious "pro" miles, instead of the usual "pseudo-pro" levels.

It was only a matter of time before I blew up again, and it came a few weeks before I was due to leave for Australia. It wasn't as drastic as the year before, but my twelfth place finish in the World Cup was a fraction of the performance level I was capable of a month before. I was tired all month before Nice and struggled to another sub par eleventh place finish there.

That didn't make the folks at IMG, the worldwide sports marketing giant that owned and organized the race, too happy. They had signed me to an agreement to secure my return to Nice earlier in the year. As the returning sixth place finisher, the offer was increased to airfare, hotel, and a huge (for me anyway) appearance fee and prize money guarantee of $3,000. I was able to receive this outrageous sum due to a bidding war IMG was involved in with another big race that was scheduled for the same day as Nice in Scottsdale, AZ. It was promoted by none other than Patrick O'Riordan—of Bermuda fame—and featured a $150,000 prize purse, double that of Nice. Patrick was using hefty appearance fees and the enticing purse to sign many of the top athletes, and soon the Nice field was looking pretty weak. I didn't want to deal with Patrick again, (not that he cared) and Nice was my favorite trip of the year, so it was right place, right time, sign here on the dotted line.

The sponsorship for the Scottsdale race fell apart and it was canceled, something that would happen to O'Riordan a few more times before he disappeared from the triathlon scene. Another example of what comes around goes around. Thanks for ignoring me in Bermuda, Patrick, and driving up my market value for Nice.

After Nice, my exhausted body picked up its first injury since college, ilio-tibial tendonitis, and I was out of running for six weeks. I returned to the circuit in August with a few solid results—third at the USTS race in Dana Point, and fifth at the Chicago Sun-Times National Championship race. 1989 was fast becoming a forgettable year, marked by mediocre sponsorship and mediocre race results.

For a pro triathlete, this spells trouble, for most of us are close to the edge of financial disaster. With nothing happening in the winter months, it's mandatory to build up a good stash of money from the season to survive and be able to train properly for the upcoming season. Summer is the time for the most of the big races, but if a triathlete extends their season, some great opportunities are available as attractive purses are offered and the fields are often lighter than in peak season.

Races scheduled after the October Ironman in Hawaii are considered late season events. Ironman is the traditional finale for most pros as a long rest is usually needed after such a hard race. The water also gets cold in North America around this time, so patching a schedule together means traveling to tropical locations or doing biathlons—whatever's out there with dollar signs on it.

I returned to Ironman, intent on making sure to finish instead of racing and bombing out, and turned in an 8 hour, 57 minute finish, good for 30th place. It was a great feeling to finish and get that accomplishment out of the way. One of the most popular questions behind asking me if I can make a living doing triathlons is if I do that Ironman thing in Hawaii. It gets pretty old to always have to answer, "Not really, I do a circuit of races at shorter distances. And there's this long race in Nice, France I do that's almost as important as the Ironman."

The Ironman wasn't that exciting; I felt I couldn't really race that distance on my preparation. In fact, very few athletes are able to really race; the rest are just trying to survive it. Ironman felt like a long workout, some people passed me going faster, and I passed some others—big deal. In shorter races, I feel more like a professional athlete, in an intense battle with my competitors and my livelihood on the line.

I hit the late season circuit again as Ironman seemed like a vacation that cost me $1,000 instead of a big pro race. I achieved some good results; fifth at the Bud Light USTS National Championships in Hilton Head, first at the New York City Biathlon, and second at the Pineapple triathlon on the Caribbean island of Antigua. Antigua was a study in contrasts—athletes were holed up in luxury condos on a beautiful private beach while the rest of the population on the island lived in primitive, impoverished conditions. Antigua was the first and only triathlon where I was almost taken out during the bike ride by a stray cow crossing the road.

When the smoke cleared on the season, it looked like I would perhaps squeak by through the winter and get ready for a bigger and better 1990 season.

21

ONE PLACE, ONE RACE—A TRIATHLETE'S ECO-
NOMIC PHILOSOPHY

The hassles and frustration of dealing with the Pioneer sponsorship, and even Edgewear, which ran into financial trouble in 1989,
and eventually went bankrupt in 1990, had taken its toll on me. I
decided to get an agent to handle my sponsorship affairs, hopefully with
more success than my first managerial relationship with Johnny G's
wife. During 1989, a training partner from the Valley, Eddie Marks,
expressed an interest in soliciting sponsorship aside from my current
deals, and achieved some success. We expanded our relationship for
1990 so that Eddie would handle all of my sponsorship affairs.

I was very comfortable with Eddie as he was my age and very
personable. Since he was new to the business, we would learn together
as we went along. The well in triathlon is pretty dry compared to other
sports, and even as Eddie left no stone unturned, there was little guaranteed salary in 1990. We even tried again to get on the Pioneer team, but
they had already solidified with mostly returnees from 1989. In my
karma file I counted this as another $12,500 down the toilet. Eddie's
persistence did secure a variety of deals where compensation was based
on bonuses paid for top three race finishes, so 1990 would be put up or
shut up time.

I decided to focus on shorter distances after my three relatively
unsuccessful performances in the long events of 1989. It would be my
first season without the specter of long races hanging over my head. It
helped my training tremendously as I became less concerned with the

arbitrary mileage numbers that conventional wisdom thought was necessary for long races, and more concerned with getting my body to go fast for an Olympic distance triathlon.

My training was just as impressive as the springs of 1988 and 1989, but much more sensible. I was putting in some great workouts, but didn't feel like I was on the edge of disaster. Andrew and I settled into an effective routine, featuring back to back hard days every Tuesday and Wednesday. Tuesday was a track workout at Pepperdine University in Malibu, and we followed it up the next day with a seven hour bike ride up 6,500 foot Mt. Gleason, north of Los Angeles. It was a brutal two days, and afterwards I would disappear and take it easy until the weekend while Andrew could beat up on some other training partners in the ensuing days. I was swimming with CLASS Aquatics in Calabasas and getting more confident my weakest event would not keep me from winning some big races in 1990.

Everything was going great in preparation for the 1990 season, except for one thing: money. The well had finally run dry, and I was basically broke with a month to go before the racing season. I had lived several months off savings from the 1989 season, but with zero sponsorship income, resources had dwindled; my back was against the wall. I was faced with a number of options, and I chose the same one that I did numerous other times in my career. The choice I took was a direct result of my economic philosophy, molded from my unique career as a pro triathlete. It is similar to a stockbroker practicing the philosophy of diversifying investments based on their career experience, or a banker with conservative financial strategies.

I call my triathlete economic philosophy, "one place, one race." It may not be very sound or shrewd, but what it means to me is that I should always keep my primary focus on my training, since the incremental rewards for better performance dwarf many of the usual means to generate a little extra income. In other words, if I take a job delivering pizzas a few nights a week, I might put 100 extra bucks in my pocket each week. According to the philosophy, the job is bound to cut into my rest and recovery time and take some focus away from my training. The effect of this is impossible to directly calculate; say for argument sake that a couple months of delivering pizzas in the off season affects my training enough to lower my finish one place in the first big race of the year. The difference in prize money of the one position near the front of a big race can easily mean $1,500 to $2,000. A couple of months of shucking pizzas would bring in far less than the place difference, so by the triathletic philosophy the pizza option loses out.

The dangers of thinking like this are obvious and numerous— it's immature, irresponsible, and far more risky than having a little guaranteed income to fall back on and perhaps provide a little balance to an obsessive life-style. The worst aspect of the one place, one race philosophy is the extra pressure it creates to perform on the race course. Everyone needs a little motivation, and money is a pretty effective one. But when you are racing to pay the rent and buy food, it adds far more stress and anxiety to an already stressful and risky occupation.

I think I have been guilty in my career of blocking out how stressful the financial pressure has been and don't realize until later the toll it has taken to have my back against the wall financially. Spring 1990 was one of those times when my back was against the wall. Two big races would kick off the season, first the St. Anthony's triathlon in St. Petersburg, Florida on April 28th, and then the following week in Australia for the World Cup event on the Gold Coast at a new shorter distance. I used my credit card to charge the flights to these races and realized that if I didn't come back with a hefty sum of money for the week, that I would be in financial ruin, with no income and large credit card debts coming due.

The lowest point came at a breakfast in Malibu one morning with fellow triathlete and Malibu resident Chris Frost. He sensed that I was a little stressed out, and when I told him of my predicament, he insisted upon giving me a $200 cash loan, payable after the season began and I won some prize money. I was so desperate I took the money, promising to pay him after the inevitable big payday looming in the near future. Even with these added concerns over my head, I was so confident of my fitness that I left for Florida calm and relaxed, with a relatively clear head.

I placed second at the St. Anthony's race and earned $1,750 in prize money. I had a poor swim, an average bike, and began the run in eighth place. I had a great run and passed everybody except Mike Pigg,

120

who won by two minutes. The race netted me almost $3,000 with sponsor bonuses included, getting my head above water but not much else. I could now cover the bills, and maybe have some change left over, but the continuation of my career was still very much in jeopardy.

Fortunately, the World Cup the next weekend had a $100,000 purse and was shortened to a 1.2-mile swim, 38-mile bike ride, and ten-mile run. The race was Australia's biggest gig, and the party was rudely crashed by the American contingent. We swept the first four places in the men's race, while the following 16 money places were filled by a dozen Aussies and a few other foreigners. Mark Allen had an amazing race, beating runner up Mike Pigg by five minutes on his way to an undefeated season. Scott Tinley and I raced neck and neck the entire day. I swam next to him and his distinctive blue wetsuit, we rode side by side the entire 38 miles, holding off a huge pack formed by the rest of the top 20. We set a fast pace on the run, but some of the Aussies out of the pack were flying and steadily closing the gap on us as the finish neared. With a mile to go, Tinley and I looked assured of finishing third and fourth. I made my second move of the day to drop him and was unsuccessful. The first one was made at the halfway mark, and Tinley responded by catching up and barking to me, "I'll let you run with me, but don't try that again." Under the circumstances, he was right; we needed to work together to set the best pace, or risk getting caught by the Aussies.

We looked at each other after he answered my last surge and decided to tie and split the prize money, since we had worked together so effectively from the gun and held on by the skin of our teeth to the top places. Scott suggested that I hold the door open for him to step across the finish line first, and in return he would also split the generous bonuses he stood to make for a top three finish.

I let Tinley out-lean me in our "sprint" finish, a photo of which ended up on the cover of Australia's *Multi-Sport Magazine* the next month. I had one of the best races of my life and was ecstatic to be taking home over $7,000 for the effort. The continuation of my career was safe, and my financial picture had suddenly changed from disastrous to healthy. One place, one race.

22

BRADLEY KABOOM

The first two races of 1990 were an indication that I had reached a high level of fitness, and was capable of winning any race I entered. I raced every chance I could over the season, mixing triathlons with biathlons, eager to cash in on all the sponsor bonuses Eddie and I had lined up. Inevitably, I would crash and burn every few races as my schedule was far too ambitious. I still wasn't deterred from heavy racing, and I ended up the season starting 25 races, a ridiculous amount. In the month of September alone, I raced six times on consecutive weekends—possibly an all time triathlon record—and finally did two races on the last weekend of the month. Just like the Cleveland/Sacramento double in 1988, I won the second race of the weekend, in Huntington Beach. Maybe I needed to double more often!

I decided to follow the 1990 Bud Light US Triathlon Series, which consisted of 11 races throughout the country, culminating with a national championship race in Las Vegas in October. The series featured a large bonus pool at the end for athletes scoring the most points in the series races. Those who made the commitment would vie for the $200,000 Coke Grand Prix bonus pool, which paid the top ten male and female point scorers on the season, including $30,000 to the winners. The Coke Grand Prix was enticing, but it meant focusing one's entire season on the Bud Light races, skipping races with big purses on conflicting dates, vying for very small prize purses at each individual series race, and paying for all travel expenses, something almost every other race assisted the pro athletes with.

Committing to the series in 1990, the result was disastrous. I did the season opener in Phoenix and finished second with a great run in a drafting marred race, which saw 35 guys get off the bike together in the lead. The race was one of the most notorious drafting scandals ever in the sport, the pack consisting of almost the entire pro field. I like to brag that I was 35th off the bike at Phoenix and in the lead at mile one of the run. Unfortunately, I was one of the 15 or so athletes they picked out of the pack to disqualify, my first and only DQ in my career for drafting.

I was pretty pissed off, because I remember minding my own business, riding with a couple other athletes at around the 20-mile mark, then hearing that noise again, the same one I heard during my first bike race at UCSB, the noise of a large pack swooping down upon us. Suddenly I was enveloped by a couple of dozen riders, and drifted to the very back of the pack to be safe and not risk a drafting call. It was so easy to ride behind such a large train that I remember sitting up on my handlebars and still holding 30 miles per hour. A couple of miles later we caught Pigg and the lead group, who earlier had a minute lead on my small group before we caught the train. I had a tremendous advantage on the ride, and never would have caught the leaders otherwise, but so did everyone, so I felt randomly picking names out of the pack to disqualify was not an acceptable solution. Instead of a decent check, some nice top three bonuses, and a good jump on the point standings, I went home with zero points, zero dollars, and a ugly mark on my clean record of never drafting.

I still followed the series and placed fifth in the next two races, in San Jose and Baltimore. The Bud Light Series races only paid four deep, so after the first three stops on the series, Phoenix, San Jose, and Baltimore, I still had zero earnings. At that point I gave up on my commitment to the series, which was a good thing. I hit two other series events in 1990, in Chicago and San Diego, and dropped out of both races exhausted from overtraining. It was obvious that I was better off focusing on one race at a time and going where the best purses were, instead of rolling the dice and hoping for good luck many times over with the Coke Grand Prix.

The biggest victory of my career came on August 26th, the same day as a scheduled Bud Light series event, at the Reebok World triathlon in Milton, outside of Toronto, Canada. It was one of those rare days where I was in the zone and felt no pain the entire race. I earned the hefty first prize of $7,000 by swimming near the leaders, quickly disposing of them early in the bike ride, then holding off Mike Pigg—something I never thought possible—to start the run with a one minute lead. You could say I was slightly pumped to have a lead off the bike in a big race, and my victory was a certainty as I turned in the fastest run split of the day. The Reebok race and a few others I did well in that season were nationally televised on cable TV, so my name was starting to get around. I was making the jump from an up-and-comer to a legitimate contender in any race. I counted myself $7,000 ahead (in that Karma file) for dropping off the 1990 series early and being able to add the Canada race to my schedule.

Other highlights included a win at the Orange County Performing Arts Center triathlon on June 3rd, where I rode by myself a couple of minutes in front of a large pack that endured controversial drafting accusations after the race. Being a victim of drafting myself so many times, it was great to be off the front and unaffected by it. The race article in *Triathlete* magazine was titled, *"Draft Dodger"* and praised my unique method of avoiding pack riding.

My personal best six victories over the season were mixed with six DNFs or jogging finishes, I guess an understandable occurrence when you have 25 starts. I concluded from my inconsistent results that 25 races was far beyond a sane amount for a single season.

23

MR. COOL IN VEGAS

Tracy and I left LA in November 1990, moving up to the scenic and remote Northern California town of Cool, yes C-O-O-L!, outside of Sacramento in the Sierra Nevada foothills gold rush country. I was totally burnt out on the traffic and hectic pace of LA. As an athlete, who could live anywhere I wanted, why the heck was I living in LA? With the exorbitant cost of living there, Tracy and I knew that it was unlikely that we would ever be able to afford a home in an area that we liked, a sobering thought. Tracy was also ready for a change, so she quit her job at the MBA School admissions office at UCLA, and we headed North.

Tracy's parents, Mary Ann and Bern Dunigan, had left Cardiff in San Diego county the previous year and discovered Cool. On our several visits there during 1990 we fell in love with the beauty of the Sierra foothills and the slower paced life-style of the rural area. I would bring my bike up whenever we visited, wake up in the morning and arm myself with a map, food, and water, and take off exploring the high Sierras, encountering unbelievable views, little or no traffic, and plenty of long challenging climbs. Sacramento was only 45 minutes away from Cool, and many foothill residents commuted to the capital daily, so we didn't feel like we were leaving civilization cold turkey and becoming rednecks. Having the urban area nearby but living out in the country felt like a good balance from the craziness of metropolitan Los Angeles.

The training was paradise; the house we rented in Cool was in a large, gate-guarded community called Auburn Lake Trails, which featured a swimming pool, small recreational lake good for summer swimming, tennis courts, golf course, and miles of horse trails winding through the community. Auburn Lake Trails is situated on the edge of the American River Canyon, which is full of dirt trails for mountain biking and running, including the historic Western States trail, passing right behind our house, where the Western States 100-mile ultra marathon run from Squaw Valley to Auburn is contested every summer.

I could run or ride in any direction, choosing the flat terrain of the Sacramento Valley to the West, the rolling hills predominant in the foothills landscape, or head up into the mountains of the high Sierra. This was a far cry from my options in LA. We had moved from Malibu to the Marina Del Rey area for the final four months until our move North, and from our house I had exactly one option for running—the Ballona Creek bike trail. The trail was adjacent to the dingy Ballona Creek, a cement tributary of the LA River, which ran through industrial areas out to the ocean, carrying the most polluted water measured anywhere along the coastline. I'd follow the bike trail out to the jetty at the end of Marina Del Rey and return home. In all other directions there were heavily-trafficked city streets undesirable for running.

The same confinement was true for bike training. If I didn't want to drive across town, I had the option of riding on the beach bike path south towards Redondo Beach, or north towards Malibu. By the time I reached interesting terrain, it was time to turn around and head down the bike path home.

In August of 1990, I was hit by a car towing a boat trailer a block from my house. When I was laying on the ground after the impact, I screamed at the car, which braked for a moment, then apparently thought better of stopping and sped away; a hit and run. The incident symbolized the frustration I felt about training in such hectic conditions, and served as the last straw for our decision to get out of LA.

I loved the new surroundings in Cool so much that I didn't even mind training alone. I had a great running partner, our new Dalmatian named Duane, whom we acquired just before the move. He proved to be an outstanding distance runner and was always motivated to run any distance at any time of day. What better training partner could I want? No complaining, no ego, always punctual, and setting a performance standard I could never equal. If I skipped a day of running, Duane would mope around and make me feel guilty.

I had proven myself to my various sponsors over the 1990 season, and Eddie was able to secure better deals for 1991. The financial struggle was diminishing, and I was able to quietly prepare and focus on the 1991 season in Cool. I couldn't wait to get introduced at races, "Formerly from Los Angeles, and now from COOL, California, Brad Kearns!" Sounded pretty Cool...

My only training partners for months were Duane for every run, friends who would visit for a couple of days, or occasional runs and rides with a neighbor in Cool, Jim Remillard. Instead of getting psyched for the season from killer workouts as my training partners usually inspired me to in LA, I was progressing slowly, at my own pace, and wondering if I would be ready when the first race rolled around in April.

I showed up for the St. Anthony's triathlon in St. Petersburg, FL, on April 28th, 1991, not knowing if I would challenge for the win or get blown away by the whole field. Not surprisingly, my swim was severely lacking, and after an average bike ride, I started the run in twelfth place, some three minutes down on the leader. It was a brutally hot and humid day in St. Petersburg, but my running felt great, and I was reeling in much of the field. At five miles I caught three guys running together and was suddenly thrust into second place, still a minute behind a barely visible Tom Huggins in the lead. Little did I know he was falling apart and would end up in the medical tent for two hours after the race. As I made the final turn for home, I was shocked to see that I had closed the gap substantially, but he struggled across the line and held on to victory by 11 seconds. It was frustrating to come that close and be denied victory, but the race was a good confidence builder for me and an indication that I would have a strong season.

Impulsively I decided to race at the Bud Light Triathlon Series opener in Phoenix, Arizona on May 19th. The Bud Light series, formerly called the Bud Light US Triathlon Series (USTS), and I were definitely enemies after my experiences in 1990. I couldn't see myself ever sacrificing my entire season, and not attending many of the sports' biggest races, for a bunch of measly purse events that I had to pay all expenses to get to. With my historic problems with consistency, it was easy to pass up the chance at that Coke Grand Prix check every year when I planned my schedule.

A dramatic example of the hazards of committing to the series belongs to Jimmy Riccitello, a veteran pro from Tucson, Arizona. Jimmy was a regular on the series every year and always a top contender for the Coke Grand Prix title. In 1989, Jimmy was close in the point-standings going into the series championship race in Hilton Head, South Carolina. The Hilton Head results counted for double points, so depending on how the race went, several athletes were capable of placing anywhere from second in the Coke Grand Prix and earning $20,000 (Scott Molina had clinched the series title before the final event), to seventh, which would only earn $1,000.

Jimmy had an outstanding race, placing second behind winner Miles Stewart of Australia, who was not in the Coke Grand Prix. His race points clinched second for him in the Coke standings, and he was looking at a $23,000 payday, $20,000 for the Coke Grand Prix, and $3,000 for his runner-up performance in the championship race.

The race was another drafting fiasco on the flat narrow roads of Hilton Head, and word came down after the race that several DQs would be issued, including each of the top five finishers in the race! Jimmy wasn't written up for drafting, but rather for swerving around a cone into the oncoming traffic lanes, an act he insisted was to avoid hitting another rider in the pack that had formed. Ironically, there is no one more adamant in the sport against drafting than Jimmy, and here he was suffering due to pack riding. The race obviously deteriorated into a farce, not due to the athletes desire to cheat, but due to the inadequate, one lane bike course on the flat island, where competitive pro athletes were bound to bunch up with no room to maneuver.

Instead of earning double points for his second place in the championships, Jimmy now had a double zero points score, which bumped him down to seventh in the series, putting his payday for the entire season at $1,000. His disqualification had cost him $22,000, the most dramatic and unjust financial loss in the history of the sport.

My placing moved from tenth to fifth after the DQs, but I felt sick to my stomach after what had happened to Jimmy. Scott Molina, ever the good sportsman, made the point in his victory speech at the awards ceremony to recognize the athletes who were unfortunate enough to get disqualified.

Not so empathic was the speech of the sixth man across the finish line that morning, a rookie pro from Georgia named Louis Murphy, who was declared the winner after the smoke cleared from the disqualifications. His speech was peppered with "I this" and "I that" as if he had really earned this great national championship victory. I left Hilton Head disgusted with the whole situation and vowed never to return to USTS races. Of course that vow lasted until I thought I could make some money from the series in 1990. Take what you can get.

Here I was in 1991, listening to Eddie tell me about the tons of bonuses lined up for Bud Light series races. Sponsors seemed to love the series for some reason as series organizers laid the PR on heavy each year, convincing most casual observers that it was the only game in town. While it was the only national series, most people failed to recognize that the pro athletes were treated indifferently compared to other races, and that the purses and quality of field, even the media coverage, were much better at other independent races on the circuit.

I figured it couldn't hurt to get my feet wet in Phoenix, an opinion shared by many pros. Each year the races early in the series have stacked pro fields as everyone ponders whether to commit to the series and the Coke Grand Prix for the year. When the point standings start taking shape and things aren't looking so promising as happened to me in 1990, entrants steadily drop off to pursue the more lucrative independent races on the circuit. By the end of the series, the Bud Light races feature the same small group of pro men and women battling amongst themselves for the first few spots on the Coke Grand Prix.

After staying in the same time zone as the leaders in the swim in Phoenix, something I was unable to do in Florida, I easily won the race with another fast run. I committed to the series on the spot, enticed by a new rule in 1991 that scored only one's best six races, plus the championships, for the Coke Grand Prix, rather than all 11 races. I figured I had just beaten all of the top series contenders in Phoenix, and if I ran into bad luck or inconsistency problems during the season, I could drop those races from scoring with the new rules.

My solo training had prepared me adequately for the beginning of the season, but more importantly, I didn't burn out when summer hit as I had in previous years. I defended my title in June at Orange County, but not from the front this time. Instead I had to erase a one minute, 45 second lead off the bike earned by Brett Rose, which took me until five miles into the run. I was nearly dead afterwards, but I felt very satisfied that I hadn't given up, even with what seemed like an insurmountable deficit, and was able to push myself as hard as I ever had in my life to achieve the victory.

I believe there are only a few races like that in the bank, where you can muster the will to push your body far beyond its normal capabilities. My legs were only sore for a couple of days afterwards, but the race took a mental toll that lasted for a long time. Sedentary people often look at endurance athletes as crazy for pushing their bodies that hard. It's not crazy or masochistic to participate in something you prepare for and enjoy doing. Racing a triathlon can often involve quite a bit of pain, but it is usually a satisfying and manageable experience if you are prepared for it.

Yes, you can go so far outside your comfort zone in a race that it can later cause severe physical and mental damage, the point where it does become crazy. Entering an ironman distance race without a long period of diligent preparation is crazy. The distances are so extreme that racing unprepared would be an exercise in futility and self-torture. In a short race, the distances are manageable even for a moderately trained person, but ignoring pain and pushing the body to a place it has never been can become crazy too.

Most people can't get to that point because they aren't at a high enough level of fitness. The body will usually shut down before we can take it to that point of no return. A professional athlete is highly trained, theoretically can ask more of their bodies in a race, and thus be more at risk of crossing the line into the danger zone where the body and psyche are damaged by the effort.

I have been there a handful of times in my life; the brain usually has enough respect and awareness of pain to give off all kinds of powerful signals to slow the body down and protect it from damage. I guess it's a gift to be able to ignore these signals and race into oblivion, but it's a gift that must be used judiciously. I can only ignore the pain and dig to the ultimate depths when the circumstances are ideal. For example, if there is not substantial money or a significant title on the line, forget it, my brain knows it's not worth it. And if I'm not contending for the win, I can also forget it; no place is worth that much pain unless it's first. The difference between first and second is astronomical, but between second and third, third and fifth, fifth and eighth, etc., is minimal.

When I closed my eyes and took off on the final lap in those high school mile races, at city semifinals with the bad Taco in my blood, in city finals trying to qualify for state, and again at the state prelims trying to qualify for finals, I was digging as deep as I ever had. In those cases, qualifying for the next week was the victory, a do or die situation, so important I was willing to accept whatever pain was in store.

At Orange County as defending champion in front of a large group of friends and family, and faced with challenging for first place or accepting second, the circumstances were sufficient to ask for a maximum effort and accept the pain I knew would result. The price I ended up paying was 32 minutes of torture over ten kilometers of running, a few days of physical discomfort and recovery afterwards, and months of training and racing with a brain that was fried and afraid to take my body anywhere near that pain level.

I put in some solid finishes at the Bud Light series over the summer, maintaining a higher level of consistency than in previous years. I was second in San Jose and Chicago, third in Baltimore and Vermont, and first in San Diego. Sure enough, I burnt out in the month of August and missed a couple of races, but with the favorable new series scoring rules, I had enough points to assume the lead going into the championships in Las Vegas on September 21st.

All I had to do in Las Vegas was finish, at worst, a few places behind my closest contender, none other than Jimmy Riccitello. I really wanted to see him win the Coke Grand Prix someday after all his years of trying and the tragedy of 1989, but I guess just not in 1991!

I rose to the occasion and had a great race on a brutally hot and hilly course in the desert outside of Las Vegas, and finished third behind Mike Pigg and Greg Welch, both nonparticipants in the Coke Grand Prix. Finishing in Vegas with the Coke Grand Prix victory was the highlight of my career, and I was able to share it with several members of my family at the finish line.

After the awards ceremony that evening, where I chugged a Coke on stage and then high-fived the CEO of Coca-Cola, Brian Dyson, we enjoyed a night of celebrating in the casinos. I was offered a little perspective on my good fortune when I was packing up my bike in the hotel room after the race. When I tried to shift the chain for packing, my shift lever for the front derailleur broke clear off the frame. Had it happened during the race, at best I would have been stuck in one gear on the hilly course, or worse the cable could have fallen into the drive train and seized up the bike, forcing me to quit (this happened to Mike Pigg in a race earlier in the season).

To think a cheap little part on my bike could have cost me $20,000 or more was pretty sobering. "But it didn't, B RAD, it *didn't*," said Eddie in the hotel room. I couldn't speak and just sat on my bed, stunned, staring at the lever dangling off the bike.

How would I have handled it? I'm sure I would have thrown the bike off of a cliff, but I doubt I would have jumped off behind it. In any event, I felt like all the bad luck and misfortune I had suffered in my career—Perth, Bermuda, Australia, the stop sign, broken pedals, Pioneer money—had finally evened itself out, my reward for keeping a positive attitude and sticking with my career during the hard times.

24

EASY STREAK

After Vegas, it felt like a huge weight had been lifted off of my shoulders. The closer it came to the time of the championships and the more likely it seemed I would win the series, the heavier the expectation became to actually do it and get it over with. In one day I was able to change my whole life-style and financial future, a prospect that weighed heavily on me in the weeks leading up to the race. Now that the pressure and expectation had culminated, I felt like I could race more freely and more for fun, and Tracy and I could shop for a house after six years of struggling to achieve financial security through the sport.

I entered, and won, three California races in September and October: Huntington Beach, Santa Cruz and a biathlon in San Jose. My running was at a point where all I had to do was be reasonably near the lead off the bike to emerge victorious. A couple of big races were still on the schedule, the national sprint championships in Florida, the World Cup series finale and Pan American championship in Ixtapa, Mexico, and finally a return to the Eilat, Israel triathlon.

I encountered my nemesis from Orange County, Brett Rose, again at the national sprint championships. I spotted him 45 seconds off the bike, and with only three miles of running to chase him, my chances were remote of stealing another victory. I took off intent on doing so, had the run of my life, and caught him at 2 1/2 miles. I felt bad, since he had again led the race the entire way, but hey, second's all right too!

I didn't need to rely on my run in Ixtapa, Mexico, for I had the ride of my life and amassed a huge lead on one of the toughest bike courses in the triathlon world. After cycling over three major climbs and descents in the intense tropical heat of Ixtapa, on treacherous roads and facing hairy traffic conditions, I survived ten boiling kilometers on foot and arrived at the finish five minutes ahead of the next competitor, by far my biggest margin of victory ever.

My satisfaction level was through the roof. I always marveled how Pigg or Allen could totally destroy entire fields of top athletes, and wondered, "What's wrong with the rest of us when someone beats us by so many minutes?" Now I could sit back and wonder, "What's the matter with the rest of them?" It was hard to imagine winning every race, and now I was actually doing it. Everything about the sport seemed easier than ever before. For years I had to fight tooth and nail in races for every place, and feel the full effect of my efforts, but now I was running on autopilot.

Training every day was automatic: just out the door and go, no wrestling with self doubt about whether I was doing the right workouts, or whether I was too tired and spiraling downward into the pit of overtraining. My racing frame of mind was simplified. Previously, my concerns would be, "Who's here? How deep is the money? Did I rest enough for this race? Did I train enough for this race?" Now, my approach was more focused on the actual race itself, "Stay with them in the swim, hammer the bike, anybody left? OK, just outrun them and win..." The only thing I had to ponder was, "why was the sport so hard for me the rest of the time?" I couldn't really answer that one, but in late 1991, I didn't care.

Israel was my sixth win in a row, and ninth of the year, and it came at the expense of Mike Pigg, who was named the 1991 Triathlete of the Year by *Triathlete* magazine. Pigg had set the standard at Olympic distance racing for years, and it was satisfying to be able to beat him in a year when he was number one. The satisfaction stemmed not from any rivalry or animosity towards him, but rather a tremendous respect for the standard of excellence he has set in the sport throughout his career. Pigg always displays good sportsmanship, and when he congratulated me after the finish in Israel, perhaps he was disappointed not to win, but he was genuinely happy for me, knowing how hard I had worked to earn the victory.

All that was left was to cut the traditional cake decorated with Hebrew salutations at the awards ceremony, together with the female winner, Karen Smyers. Karen and I got to joke about how we were good luck for each other as we finished our seasons as the winning pair at the national sprint in Florida, then in Ixtapa, and again in Israel. After the race, Tracy and I joined Mike Pigg, his wife Marci, and Karen and her husband Mike King, for a week-long guided tour of Israel, a most excellent, historic, and educational adventure.

When we arrived home from Israel, my body told me what it thought of all the racing and traveling, and I was totally exhausted. I had started 44 races over the past two years, and coupled with the stress, although positive, of doing well, I was in need of some serious rest.

25

PIGG AND THE MIATA

My head had swelled after 1991 as I was piling up the TV and magazine coverage from racing, and Eddie was able to convince some sponsors to pay me a salary instead of basing everything on race performance bonuses. Tracy and I moved into a house we purchased in Auburn, and I was getting used to the idea of a more secure, higher profile career as a triathlete. I was presumptuous enough to think that I had my training program wired, and my main concern became how I would be able to beat Pigg in 1992 as certainly it would be he and I battling for supremacy the whole season, picking up where we left off in Israel.

I fought a cold for an entire month after coming home from Israel, and when I commenced training again in January, I still found myself exhausted. To fight a cold for that long and to still be exhausted after a month's rest was unusual, but I plugged away, hoping I would get my energy back by getting in shape. In reality I had taken my body to such a point where, after six years of hard training and racing nearly year-round, I was in dire need of an extended vacation from training. It was either that or my body would take one against my will at some point in the future. I probably needed two or three months completely off, but I felt I couldn't do that because I had to prepare for the early races of the 1992 season where much was expected of me.

I did the team thing again, signing for the season with Team DeGeorge, based out of Connecticut and backed by a multi-millionaire businessman named Peter DeGeorge. Peter was a fan of triathlon and a recreational participant while his wife Mary was the top amateur in the world in her age group as well as a competitive pro biathlete at the age of 40. The team had formed a few years prior when Peter decided to sponsor a few athletes in the Connecticut area, and also in the South Florida area where he had a second home. It soon mushroomed to a team of some 15 athletes, including six professional competitors, three male and three female.

The team was a philanthropic gesture on Peter's part, and the expectations from our sponsor were minimal. We were required to attend two team meetings over the year, actually lavish party weekends, one in Florida over the winter, and one in Connecticut over the summer. Each gathering placed a heavy emphasis on fun and games with all the toys imaginable, beautiful accommodations (the DeGeorge's hosted almost the entire team at their new home in Connecticut), great meals, a little training, and the annual DeGeorge triathlon in Connecticut. (A decent pro purse was provided by the title sponsor, and Team DeGeorge members were the only pros in attendance!)

I felt like this was Team JDavid all over again, only this time I was one of the lucky pros to be a part of it. I was offered a generous salary for title sponsorship, and I would still be allowed to place smaller logos of other sponsors on my clothing, increasing the value of those contracts. The team had no desire to control my training, race schedule, or dealings with other sponsors. Eddie secured a few other good contracts, and in one year my salary for racing as a pro triathlete jumped from next to nothing to earning a decent living.

My results and notoriety had increased my value to sponsors, but with that came increased pressure and responsibility to them. Most of the pressure is self imposed as my sponsors have rarely been difficult or demanding in regards to my race performances, but there is always an implied expectation to perform at a high level if they are paying you accordingly. Conversely, with race bonus contracts, there is little of this pressure since no results means no compensation from the sponsor. A company is taking very little risk in offering a bonus contract; if the athlete flops, the company is only out whatever free product they provided. When an athlete turns in good results, the company pays for what they get in terms of exposure, and everyone is happy. But when guaranteed cash is changing hands, this is a budgetary decision for a company that is reviewed annually. If inadequate results are attained over the year, the athlete can usually kiss the money good-bye when it's time for renewing contracts and figuring new budgets.

I was certainly willing to take the trade-off of extra pressure and expectation for a salary. That pressure is nothing compared to having no sponsors and racing to make ends meet with prize money. I enjoy having more value and responsibility to my sponsors. Doing things like appearing at a sponsor's booth at a race expo or trade show, shooting print ads or promotional videos, or getting up at sunrise for a week to shoot the Hind sportswear catalog (wearing tank tops and shorts on freezing winter mornings in the mountains to photograph the spring clothing line) was hard work, but it is the only way to become truly valuable to a sponsor.

Race results can only get you so famous. Most athletes, even in major sports, gain as much notoriety through the power of commercial endorsements, exposure that is paid for by the sponsors and could never be achieved solely through competitive efforts. Michael Jordan and Andre Agassi would certainly be extremely famous if Nike, et al., didn't exist, but their print and television commercials created a worldwide image for them, far exceeding the scope of their competitive efforts.

As my preparations for the 1992 season continued through the spring, I was getting very fit, but it felt like it was coming at the expense of my health. There is a huge difference between health and fitness, and when errors are made in training, they can come at the expense of one another. When an athlete overtrains in pursuit of competitive fitness, the body soon breaks down, either biomechanically with an injury, with a suppressed immune system, hormonal irregularities, or other problems that result in a lowered state of health. The only answer to overtraining is rest, where health can return, but it comes at the expense of fitness.

The challenge is to build and maintain both constantly, which means monitoring all the stress the body is put under while attempting to balance it with an equal amount of rest. When too much stress is placed on the body, no matter what kind, the body is susceptible to breakdown and a loss of health. Most of us ignore the positive, enjoyable stress we place on the body when determining how much rest we need to balance ourselves. Exercise is often discussed as a great "balance" to a stressful workday and hectic modern life-style. This is true in a number of important ways, but training is still a physical stress and must be considered such when weighing one's hypothetical balance scale of stress and rest.

When stress from work, family, and everyday life rises to high levels, a corresponding reduction in training is necessary to maintain a healthy balance. I once read a study that showed getting married to be among the most stressful events in a person's life—right up there with death in the family, loss of job, serious illness, etc. Hopefully a wedding is a happy occasion, but it produces profound changes in one's life and is thus highly stressful. Similarly, the stress of going from an obscure athlete to suddenly winning races and gaining notoriety, or competing for and winning the relatively high stakes of the Coke Grand Prix, are positive and desirable, yet stressful situations. Continuing to race, and win, those remaining races in 1991 showed me that my fitness was high, but so was my stress level, which eventually affected my health with an extended winter illness.

I was able to put in some great workouts in the spring of 1992, highlighted by a weekly seven hour "death ride." The death ride was a 100-mile route leaving from my house in Auburn every Tuesday and climbing in and out of several river canyons in the high Sierra, a total of 12,000 feet of climbing. I had regular customers each week as word spread to the triathletes in the area, many of whom were accustomed to riding in the flatlands of the Sacramento Valley and rarely venturing higher than the foothill communities like Auburn for hill riding. The terrain and length of the death ride had a way of completely altering one's perspective upon completion.

In the middle of the ride, at the bottom of the American River Canyon high in the Sierra, there is a 3 1/2-mile stretch of road, snaking right up the face of the steep canyon wall, which climbs 2,000 feet up to Ralston Ridge. I named the section the Corkscrew Wall as the road winds in a spiral fashion unrelentingly up the canyon wall until it finally offers a merciful break upon reaching the ridge line.

Dealing with the ascents out of the canyons, conquering the Corkscrew Wall, having no food or water available for almost four hours through the national forest area, and then facing the final insult, a 2 1/2-

mile climb up to Auburn from the American River at the very end of the ride, leaves you with a tremendous sense of satisfaction.

After a death ride, my perspective towards training totally changes. That little hill that I loved to complain about at the end of a regular 50-mile loop elicits nary a second thought after taking the mind and the body successfully through a challenge far greater. Sometimes I think for all the physical benefits of a long difficult ride, the mental benefits might even be more significant. Completing the ride, concentrating for so long, and making it through the inevitable ups and downs, is an ideal form of mental training for an athlete.

Many question the benefits of such long training rides when preparing for a 40 kilometer bicycle leg in an Olympic distance triathlon, but I think the confidence and altered perspective gained is bound to translate into reduced apprehension, better concentration and increased confidence when competing over 40 kilometers. The mind says, "40 kilometers? We just did four times that in training, with hills far worse than this race course. What a piece of cake. I'm just going to hammer the whole way." When the mind looks at a challenge that way, it enhances instead of interferes (as it would if the athlete had any apprehension about the distance or difficulty of the course) with a maximum effort by the body. Meanwhile the body has developed some pretty strong legs to pump the pedals for those 40 kilometers.

The only side effect of these consistent weekly death rides was that I suffered from severe lulls in energy in between periods of good training. My health was unable to keep pace with my fitness, and I was heading for a disastrous crash come summer.

I did have the juice for the first couple of races, and finally got a win at the season opening St. Anthony's in Florida, after two straight years as runner-up. It was a good time to win as the race was featured in *Triathlete* magazine and a photo of me leading on the run graced the cover. I had finally reached my ultimate goal of getting on the cover of *Triathlete* after six years of trying! I told people when the magazine hit the newsstands that I could retire now and be happy. Not really true, but the cover felt like an important milestone for me. Underneath my cool exterior, I was a hard-core tri-geek who had saved every issue of the magazine since I began competing in 1984.

140

After placing third the weekend after St. Anthony's in St. Croix, Virgin Islands, I returned home to prepare diligently for what I considered the most important race of my life, the June 1st Mazda/ Orange County Performing Arts Center triathlon, my "hometown" (Southern California), personal favorite race, where I was two-time defending champion. The name of the race was changed in 1992 to add Mazda to the title as they came aboard as a major sponsor by offering 1992 Mazda Miata automobiles to the male and female race winners.

I was excited about the changes in Orange County where the stakes for winning suddenly shot up from $2,000 to an $18,000 new car. The race had always been a big time corporate affair with heavy PR efforts and media coverage. As the defending champ, I flew down to Orange County twice before the race to speak at a sponsors' luncheon and press conference, give pre-race training clinics for Mazda employees and race registrants, and do a taped commentary previewing the race course for the television program. ("This brutal hill you see in the background comes at the five-mile mark on the run. I made my move right here last year to catch leader Brett Rose en route to my second consecutive victory.")

I wanted nothing more than to win the Miata and knew I would have to beat Mike Pigg, the best cyclist in the sport, and Greg Welch, the best runner in the sport, to get it. With that in mind, I set out to improve my running and cycling enough in one month so that the sum of my parts would equal a whole new Miata at the finish line June 1st. A week after St. Croix, I won a very hilly 10K race in Auburn in 33 minutes, 15 seconds, a great time considering the course. The following weekend, I had one of my best workouts ever: four repeat miles on the track in under five minutes sandwiched by four times ten minutes of hard cycling on the stationary turbo-trainer I set up track-side. The workout felt easy, and I felt great the following day, so I went out and intelligently rode 80 miles.

The next morning I woke up, two weeks out from the race, feeling like I was hit by a truck. I had fallen off of the same dreaded cliff as I had before my early season races of '88 and '89; my adrenal glands were probably shrunk to the size of pinheads! This final-hour fatigue caused a total panic, and I still felt horrible when I left for Orange

County the Thursday before the Sunday race.

At the first buoy offshore in the swim, I knew my race was over. I had nothing and was soon dropped by all the contenders. I rode the bike as hard as I could to no avail, and then jog/walked through the run, exhausted, sharing last place honors with Kerry Classen, a young pro who also had an off day. Greg Welch ran away with the race and drove away with the Miata, while Carol Montgomery of Canada edged Michellie Jones of Australia for the female victory.

I was totally exhausted after the race, and the feeling continued for the next two months, causing me to miss many important summer races. It looked like my prediction for the season, Pigg and I battling it out for supremacy in the short-course triathlon world, was not quite playing out as I had imagined. By late August, I had pulled it together enough to turn in some decent results, like fifth at Chicago Sun Times, and third in Beijing, China, which qualified me to race in the ITU (International Triathlon Union, the official worldwide governing body of triathlon) World Championships in Muskoka, Ontario, Canada on September 12th.

The Worlds featured a huge field of over 100 professionals, and soon deteriorated, predictably, into a pack riding affair on the narrow roads around the rural resort area of Muskoka. I was feeling great on the bike, I thought, although it's impossible to really tell when riding in a pack, and I got off the bike in the lead, with about 25 others. I felt terrible on the run; the air was very cold, and my body just didn't seem to want to wake up. I had to let the top five go in the early stages, soon drifted out of the top ten, but then got a second wind and gutted out a fifth place finish, the first North American finisher. I would have been quite pleased with a fifth place in World's a month after being on the couch exhausted and unable to train, but I felt like the race was a farce due to the bike ride, and my run was nowhere near the form I displayed in 1991.

Sometimes I have race finishes that look better on paper, and I get more attention than I deserve, just as I have great races that go relatively unrecognized for whatever reason. A race might have a great title like "World Championships," but if the field is weak (due to limits on entrants from any one country in championship races, for example) or the race is marred by drafting on the bike, it loses some of its value to me and other athletes, yet often remains important in the eyes of the public. Conversely, a race like Israel is hardly known in America, due to its remote location and very late season date, but beating the Triathlete of the Year and winning $5,000 made it seem far more significant to me than struggling to a fifth place in the "World Championships." This doesn't mean Eddie and I didn't pump the angle for all it was worth as we made sure sponsors and everyone else who would listen knew of my "Great race, fifth at Worlds, first North American..."

The rest of 1992 was a downer. I got tired again after Worlds and suffered from stomach problems. I only raced twice more, a tenth at the Las Vegas Bud Light Championships (I made $300 instead of the $30,000 the year before), and then a fourth behind the Euro boys in Eilat, Israel. By the end of the season, any residual head-swelling from 1991 had subsided. 1993 was looking like a comeback year for Brad and his 1986 Isuzu Trooper with 100,000+ miles on it, instead of my fantasy of winning another Miata in Orange County in 1993.

26

BRAD WHO?

I began preparations for 1993 intent upon erasing the memory of my fatigue-ridden struggle of 1992. Everyone's allowed an off year, right? I had the urge to return to long distance racing again after a three-year absence, so I signed up for the New Zealand Ironman on March 7th. With so much time off the previous year, I figured I could maintain training through the winter without suffering any ill effects and be fit when the early race date arrived.

My training was going relatively well, but I was gun shy and reluctant to push myself over the edge. My training schedule wasn't demanding, yet it still didn't feel as easy as it had in 1990 and 1991. I had become accustomed to struggling in training and suffering bouts of exhaustion lasting a few days to a week where I had to cease exercising. The memory of my free-spirited beginnings in the sport, hammering away with reckless abandon and feeling great, were growing more and more distant.

The more difficult things got in the present, the more I would think back to the state I was in over the winter of 1986-87, or over the 1991 season. I had far less confidence, and any mistakes I made in training would cause me to crash. I longed to return to my free-spirited days, but instead I became more compulsive and tense about every aspect of my career.

This contradicts the stereotypical image of the champion athlete—leading a highly focused, strictly regimented life-style while the also-rans are thought to be less focused and more likely to been seen staying out late at a bar or something. When I achieved my best success, I was laid back and led a more balanced life. Staying out late and losing sleep, eating something that was off the training diet, or doing any activity that interfered with training or racing, (like sight-seeing before a race instead of laying in bed all day resting), didn't stress me out as much as when I was struggling. This attitude magnified my struggles.

Either way, there is a snowball effect. Success breeds more success. The increased confidence and positive reinforcement make it easier to remain on track and duplicate top performances. Conversely, failure and struggle often cause everything to go into a tailspin—confidence, motivation, stress level—which breeds more failure and prolongs the struggle.

We read about how powerful the mind is for peak athletic performance, but I think many people fail to realize that you can't fake confidence no matter how hard you psych up, visualize, or focus. The mind/body connection can mean many things—you can get more out of the body with the mind's help, but if the body is not ready, the mind will know. When the going gets tough, it will usually give up. As Johnny G liked to say, "The psych ends when the pain begins." In an endurance sport like triathlon, this is prophetic. You can work yourself into a frenzy at the swim start, huffing, puffing, screaming, visualizing yourself as a dolphin, getting totally psyched, but if you are not trained well enough, the pain will arrive and you will get left behind. Maybe it helps to psych up for a football game, but without adequate preparation, the banner smashing, screaming huddle, helmet bashing, massive psych-up will be a waste of energy. A weaker team will still get blown off the field.

I believe it is imperative to get the mind in the proper state for a peak performance, through visualization, positive self-talk, etc., but only when it is pure, when the individual truly feels it without having to force it. When training is going great, it's difficult to not feel confidence, and the positive self-talk and daydreams about victory come automatically without having to be conjured up. The experience I had visualizing my January 1987 Desert Princess victory with Johnny G was powerful because I knew I was ready for the race of my life. The visualization was natural, unforced, and heartfelt. If I had attempted to do that before the February Desert Princess race, for example, when I was stressed out and sick and not ready for a peak performance, the experience would have been more forced and far less powerful or effective. Confidence is pretty high on the list of determining factors for success, but it is something you cannot steal or fake, it has to arrive naturally in your consciousness through the positive results that occur from hard work.

Thinking back to past heroics and pondering the de-evolution of my career was difficult to accept. There is much talk and evidence in endurance sports of growing stronger with age and experience; I felt the opposite was happening to me. This was not a good feeling in the eighth year of my pro career. After dedicating so many years of my life to the sport, the rewards need to increase, both financially and spiritually, to justify continuing on. I wanted to continue racing and was obligated to for my sponsors, so I had no choice but to plug along and do the best I could, feeling like I was running on less than all cylinders.

I flew to New Zealand with some decent preparation under my belt, and by the halfway point on the run, I had moved into fifth place. Soon after, I bonked hard and then my knee started to go. Ironically, things worsened right as the race course passed under the finish banner at the 16-mile mark. The route then headed out and back along the coast before returning again to the finish. As I hobbled past the start finish area in seventh place and fading fast, I noticed the rows of tables stocked with food for race finishers and the dozens of massage therapists standing beside their tables waiting for the onslaught. I took a hard left off the course and headed for the lunch tables, then a long massage. I figured shuffling ten more miles and risking a more severe injury to my knee was hardly worth the possible chance of staying in the top ten and taking home a big fat check for $300. After the race, my appetite for long-distance racing had been satiated for good.

In the three seasons when I completely avoided long races, I often wondered how I could have fared. I competed regularly on the short course against many of the top ultra-distance competitors, and with a few years to dull my memory of the nature of ultra-distance training and racing, I started to speculate favorably about my potential upon returning to ultras. I was enticed financially by the Ironman World Series, a sort of ultra-distance Coke Grand Prix, which offered a substantial bonus pool for points scored in one's three best Ironman races over the season, including the championships in Hawaii. The individual Ironman events all had substantial purses, enough to get me to the starting line in New Zealand, but I guess not the finish line.

I came away from the race not even disappointed that I had dropped out. At one point late in the bike ride, when I was still feeling great, I realized that I was nevertheless losing interest in the race. I wasn't losing the ability to concentrate or focus due to fatigue, but losing it out of boredom. Six hours felt like plenty of time to race, thank you—unfortunately I still had a few more hours to go until the finish. When you lose even a little of the will to continue and finish in an Ironman race, you are doomed.

I realized my temperament is suited for the Olympic distance. Ironman races are so long they require shutting off many of my natural competitive instincts in favor of concentrating on pacing to ensure a successful finish. At the other end of the spectrum, I learned from high school that the mile was too intense, nerve racking, and painful for me to tolerate. After experiencing both extremes, I settled on a happy medium and vowed to be an Olympic distance specialist the rest of my triathlon career.

A part of me felt sad that I was turning my back on such a huge part of the sport. How do I explain that I was a professional triathlete, yet didn't even take part in the sports ultimate race, the Hawaii Ironman? Another part of me knew exactly what the Ironman was about and how difficult it was to prepare for and compete as a pro. I was content with the fact that I made a conscious choice, that the sacrifice required to be competitive (missing short distance races that I had a much better chance of winning, juggling the extra training necessary to be competitive at both distances, and suffering for eight plus hours instead of a couple) was not worth it. I had no regrets about it and had enough respect for the athletes who excelled in ultras that I would never scan race results thinking, "He got top ten at the Ironman? God, I killed him at that Olympic distance race!"

After New Zealand, training continued to be mediocre. I wasn't able to even train hard enough to break down like I had in prior years. This also produced mediocre race results, such as unsuccessfully defending my title at St. Anthony's Tampa Bay with a pathetic ninth place, then backing that up with another ninth at St. Croix. These were some of my worst "fresh" races (where I had no excuse like being exhausted or overtrained and was able to race according to my fitness level at that time) in years, but I still tried to maintain a positive attitude.

I did get a glimpse of the return to the zone, but just for one hour on May 23rd at the DCA Atlanta Sprint triathlon. Sprint is definitely my best distance, and unfortunately it is not contested very often on the circuit. My strengths tend to be speed and power, due to my physiological makeup, regardless of the training I put in.

These genetic traits possibly explain why I have trouble handling high mileage training and long distance racing, which rely on aerobic endurance as opposed to speed and power. My athletic background of track and cross-country featured races of two minutes to 15 minutes in length, where the entire race is very intense and heavily anaerobic in nature. From possessing these strengths one can infer that I have a higher proportion of fast twitch muscle fibers in my legs, which work effectively anaerobically (without oxygen) for short periods of time. Triathlon and other endurance sports rely heavily on the slow twitch muscle fibers, which work effectively aerobically (with oxygen) for long periods of time without fatiguing.

Anyone's muscles can learn to adapt with specific training for an event like triathlon. However, we are all limited in our potential by various genetic factors like the percentage of fast to slow twitch muscle fibers. Carl Lewis or Florence Griffith Joyner would never be competitive in endurance sports. Their muscles are extremely powerful and are able to generate great speed for short periods of time. But no amount of training will change their essential genetic makeup as sprinters. The same is true for most of us that would never be able to run a decent 100 meters or dunk a basketball no matter how hard we practiced.

Relative to many of my triathlon peers, the faster and shorter the race, the more advantage I have. These same advantages are apparent on race courses that feature short steep hills requiring tremendous power to negotiate, courses like Orange County, Ixtapa, Mexico, or the Atlanta course through the Stone Mountain State Park, not coincidentally the site of my best races.

Generally speaking, athletes excel on courses and over distances that cater to their unique genetic traits. My training partner Andrew and I are genetic opposites; he thrives on high mileage and excels at long hill climbs on a bike like few in the history in the sport. Strength and power are his shortcomings; years of diligent work in the weight room did nothing to change his hopelessly skinny physique, and his back and shoulder muscles regularly gave out from heavy training. With me, if I look at a weight, I start to get too bulky. Yet, I could never handle the amount of aerobic work Andrew thrived on, nor stay with him on long climbs. He ran the mile in high school much slower than I did, but he can be totally out of shape and hang with me on any hill in training—even when I'm in peak form.

I think it is crucial for all athletes to be aware of their inherent strengths and weaknesses, and to learn the type of training that is best for them. It calls to mind the story of my training discussions in 1988 with Dave Scott and Mark Allen. How was it possible that these top athletes could both excel in the same event with seemingly totally different training philosophies? They had discovered, through trial and error, what types of workouts their bodies needed most, something every athlete needs to do.

It's easy to pick up a book, an article, or listen to a coach or fellow athlete for ideas on training. Newcomers to a sport have no choice but to learn from others. But it is important to always have your eyes open to how the body feels and adapts to your training. The next step is to learn from your mistakes, and successes, and revise your training program accordingly. In a sport as challenging and with as many variables as triathlon, this is a constant learning process. I don't think there is such a phenomenon as having one's training "wired." What once worked effectively may not in the future due to changes in other variables—age, life-style changes like moving to a new environment, new job, new relationship, people racing faster, etc.

My star faded again after Atlanta as I returned to training struggles and poor or mediocre finishes. I was a non-factor in Orange County again, watching Mike Pigg and Michellie Jones win their Miatas. I plugged along on the circuit, somehow making the USA team for the World Championships on August 22nd in Manchester, England. My 24th place finish ranked up there with the lowest points in my career, only to be rivaled the following week when I dropped out of the Chicago Sun-Times race 200 meters into the swim, suffering from a panic attack and unable to breathe. I'm sure my attack was caused by extreme fatigue as it was the fourth race in four weeks, coming on the heels of two difficult and disappointing races in Europe. I was in no condition to race, and I was in such a funk at the time I guess I didn't realize it when I boarded the plane to Chicago.

The only thing to do after hitting bottom was to step away and take one of my now patented breaks from the sport. I went up to Andrew's home in Lake Tahoe where we glued ourselves to the couch for a few days, commiserating about both being at the nadir of our careers (Andrew was 50th at the Worlds). At the end of the week, I stepped out the door and had one of the best runs of my life with Andrew and our swim coach Bud, who was notorious for pushing the pace. We hammered for an hour and a half in the mountains, covering much of the same course as the World's Toughest triathlon. I felt like I was floating the whole way, and at the end of the run my whole attitude and perspective on the sport changed from "poor me" to "where's the next race?" Pretty fragile psyche, right? Hey, whatever it takes!

All that racing had brought me to a high fitness level, and once I backed off and recovered from the hectic schedule of travel and racing, I could feel the benefits. The next time out of the gate I placed a solid third in Acapulco, Mexico, unfortunately inventing yet another way to get disqualified from a race. The race was oppressively hot, and I opted not to wear my racing singlet during the run, since the race number pinned to the front of the shirt tore off when I attempted to put it on. Without a race number, the shirt served no official purpose, and I waited until approaching the line to display my number in my hands to the officials. It is against the rules to not display your number on the front of your body during the entire run segment, but circumstances like having the number tear off clothing happens on occasion, and usually nothing is thought of it. Usually... Oh well, at least I was in shape and felt good about my return to fitness.

My next two races, both in October, were also solid performances, a second place in the Santa Cruz Sentinel triathlon, followed by a fifth at the ITU World Cup finale and Pan American championships in

St. Thomas, Virgin Islands. The results were encouraging in the context of my difficulties over the past two seasons, yet far below the standards I had set in previous years. Maintaining energy in training continued to be a struggle. I resigned to the fact and just tried to do the best I could. Instead of having the whole package on race day as I always would during peak periods, my races featured inconsistencies in the various segments, the unexplainable phenomena that plagues many triathletes. For example, in Acapulco, I had a miserable bike ride and a brilliant run. In Santa Cruz and St. Thomas, great rides and lousy runs.

I would always chuckle to myself at athletes during our ceremonial post-finish BS sessions when they would comment, "Gosh, my bike legs felt great today, but I had nothing on the run." I never had the privilege of experiencing such mysteries of the human body—either I had it all or I was totally wasted and had nothing. Now I could empathize with this feeling, but was even more bewildered as to the cause. Overtraining in that particular event? Perhaps, but whenever I overtrained, I suffered from general bodily fatigue; it wasn't like I ever felt overtrained on the run and could go out and have a great bike ride. Perhaps my system is so fragile that I could never get to the point in training where the muscles specific to the various sports became exhausted before the overall body. It's one of the frustrating mysteries of triathlon.

My season ended prematurely after St. Thomas as I crashed on my mountain bike and cracked a couple of ribs, making it too painful to continue to swim. I think it was a merciful end as I was totally worn out after the St. Thomas race. The island consists almost entirely of steep hills, and the bike and run courses pretty much covered each one of them it seemed, all in the tropical heat of the Caribbean. Thus I closed the book on 1993 on somewhat of a high note with a fifth place in a big race, yet my body's repeated failures in training left me concerned and apprehensive about the future of my career.

Everyone's allowed a couple off years, right? Well, not in triathlon. My glory days of 1991 had faded entirely, and new stars like Brits Simon Lessing and Spencer Smith, both in their early 20s, had arrived on the triathlon scene to share the spotlight with the veterans like Pigg, and Australians Greg Welch and Brad Beven. A whole new crop of Americans were coming up and asserting themselves, guys like Wes

Hobson, Bill Braun, and Nate Llerandi. Although I had been able to maintain a respectable final USA ranking at Olympic distance of sixth in both 1992 and 1993, in triathlon the difference between that and the top is like night and day. There is not enough money to comfortably support more than a handful of pros, and my comfort days were temporarily over as my three best sponsors for many years all decided to spend their money elsewhere for the 1994 season.

I had tons of great products from a variety of sponsors, and Eddie set me up with some nice bonus incentive contracts to replace the salaried agreements, but I was basically starting from ground zero in 1994, my ninth year as a full-time professional. I suddenly felt like an old man at 29, getting pushed out of the limelight, and perhaps the sport, before my time by virtue of going too slow on the race course.

There exists a phenomenon in the triathlon world with the media and sponsors where familiar veteran athletes are pretty much ignored, or simply accepted as cogs in the machine. Most everybody in the sport knew my name and my career highlights, but a fifth here and a third there by eight year veteran Brad Kearns is understandably old news. The attention always goes to the winners, but also to each athlete who is able to make that breakthrough and arrive on the scene.

Every pro gets their fifteen minutes of fame in triathlon, and it comes at that race or races where no one's heard of you, but you suddenly are right there with the big boys or girls in the results. A thorough background check is done, your story is told to everyone, and soon everyone knows all about the new arrivals. Then it's time to sit back and see if the new flashes in the pan will be just that, or if they can continue their rise, unseat the true legends of the sport on occasion, and be able to do it over a significant period of time. Most everyone fails at this, since there are only a few legends. The reason there are so few is that the legends win all the races.

Anything short of winning consistently puts the typical pro triathlete in a situation of receiving moderate recognition and moderate income. Before you know it several years have gone by, everyone knows your name, but nobody gets excited about anything you do unless they are your family members or you pull off a big win (which some damn good pros never achieve). If it sounds pretty depressing, it's not, because the true rewards for doing anything have to come from within, and racing in relative obscurity is something almost everyone needs to accept and come to terms with as part of the game in triathlon.

For me, I can readily accept it and even use it as fuel for the fire. I am not bitter towards a sponsor who drops me like a hot potato as much as I am not abashed at taking whatever I can get when I am on top. I don't feel slighted when no one interviews me after a fourth place finish just as I don't have any qualms about getting mobbed when I win. For a long time I was bitter about the top-heavy distribution of sponsor dollars, prize money and appearance fees on the pro circuit. Then I realized, perhaps from being on both sides of the coin, that the top finishers and the big names are what make the race, or a company's promotional campaign, and they will be paid accordingly in a free market economy. It's not like anyone gets a head start in the race, so who can be bitter? The sport, for all its flaws, has to be ten times fairer than moving up the ladder in corporate America, a ladder I climbed off many years ago.

Often I am quoted in the media as saying that winning means everything to me in this sport. I mean this not be arrogant, but to emphasize that hoping for or accepting anything less as an ultimate goal makes the sacrifice of dedicating my life to the sport not worth it. This doesn't mean I will be unhappy with not winning every race since that is not realistic. It means that I need to focus on that as justification for continuing my career. If my aspirations were anything less, I would just race as an amateur and enjoy the training and competition almost as much while pursuing another rewarding career.

I do the sport primarily for myself. It's a very selfish pursuit. One way to give something back to everyone who supports me is to win. Everyone loves a winner, in life and particularly in sports, and the attention, glory, and boost to the ego that winning provides must not be understated due to political correctness.

Mark Allen has a great passage in his book, *Total Triathlete,* where he says he knows he is in a good place spiritually when he is able to be happy when others are recognized even if he is not:

"I sometimes imagine that I'm in a crowd of world class athletes receiving awards for excellence. As the awards are presented, everyone claps. All the athletes in the room receive an award but me, even though I had a fantastic season. I'd be in my ultimate place within myself if, after not receiving an award, I could be sincerely happy for everyone else. My praise wouldn't have to come from an external source. I should be happy with myself."

This is a wonderful place to aspire to, probably out of reach for most people. However, if you're one of the people who gets called up on stage to receive an award, it is OK to take that energy from admirers and absorb it and bask in it. This is usually thought of as getting a big head, but getting a big head and maintaining a healthy balance and perspective on your achievements and your life are not mutually exclusive.

It's worse to never be happy with your performance or yourself, no matter how great your achievements are. The most disgusting example I have ever seen of this came from American swimmer Rick Carey, the gold medalist in the backstroke in the 1984 Olympics in Los Angeles. He was heavily favored to win and was looking to set a world record to top it off. He won easily, but in a time that was subpar for him, no world record. He was so upset he sulked, for all the world to see, while standing on the victory podium with an Olympic gold medal around his neck, listening to the national anthem! If you can't be happy with an Olympic gold medal, what's it all worth?

It looked like I was at a serious crossroad. I could either resurrect my career, by returning to the winners circle, or fade away and earn a one way ticket into the real world with anything less than a great season. Rather than feel a tremendous pressure as I had in past years when my back was against the wall financially, I accepted my predicament and decided to do my best and accept whatever happened. Perhaps almost a decade on the circuit changed my perspective and mellowed me out. I knew that logically I had many more years left in me for racing and that my mind had been trained to the point where I could tolerate all of the pain and pressure that the sport doles out. What remained to be seen was whether my body could hold up to the challenge.

27

DO OR DIE...AGAIN?

The only thing I truly feared in my career was that my body would fall apart despite my best intentions as I pursued competitive fitness. From this position of no confidence, I made what turned out to be a fatal mistake by altering some major time-tested training strategies to see if something new would work in 1994.

Ever since my experimentation with Dave Scott's intense training program in 1988, I believed that for me the best strategy was to minimize high-intensity training and focus on building and maintaining an aerobic base. My physiological characteristics, possessing natural strength and speed and the tendency to break down easily, led me to adopt this philosophy. My best training and racing has always occurred when I paid close attention to my body and took great care not to overstress it. This approach always manifested itself in a very loosely organized, low-intensity training schedule.

This contrasts the typical athletic philosophy of being consistent and sticking to a strict training schedule to improve fitness. Whenever I tried to follow a schedule, I ended up going against my instincts and forcing my body through workouts for the sake of honoring the schedule. This was particularly true for intense workouts. My body is rarely ready to race—15 times in an entire year always feels like plenty. A training schedule chock full of workouts that rivaled races in intensity always wore me out, probably because I had difficulty telling my mind it wasn't a race, to just calm down and do a hard workout.

The great majority of my track workouts have been great,

because my mind goes bonkers when I step onto the track and primes my body for a peak race effort—even on a Tuesday morning with no one in the stands. The times look great in the log book, and they help to psych me up, but I feel they come at the expense of race performance somewhere down the line.

I knew I could race successfully on an unstructured, comfortably paced training program, but the feeling was clouded over by my lack of confidence from two years of poor racing. So what did I do? I decided to junk the foundation of my training for eight years—long rides and runs in the hills, which build a great aerobic base, in favor of a new stricter program featuring a regular dose of high intensity training. My rationale was that the long workouts—few Olympic distance triathletes make a habit of seven hour training rides—was perhaps part of the cause of my energy lulls. This theory was further supported by the overwhelming lack of scientific evidence supporting a correlation between slow over-distance training and high intensity race performance.

I've read and digested tons of studies and theories from noted experts in human performance who all conclude that the best way to become competent at something is by specific preparation. That is, to run a fast 10K or ride a fast 40K, you have to frequently practice at the pace you wish to race. The need for building an aerobic base is always emphasized, but often it's in terms of just a base for faster training. It all makes perfect sense, except for one thing: there is just as overwhelming an amount of anecdotal evidence from world class athletes in triathlon, and the three individual sports of which it is comprised, that aerobic, over-distance training is emphasized far more than recommended by scientific theories. The best swimmers, pro cyclists, track and road runners, and top triathletes are out there putting in the miles, carrying out the great majority of their training at far below race pace. What gives? Both schools of thought have credibility—just like Dave Scott, Ironman champion and exercise physiologist, and Mark Allen, Ironman champion and Zen Master, both have for their differing training philosophies.

I had to make a choice, so I factored in my own personal experiences (the most important factor of all), the repeated injuries and illnesses from high intensity college running, and the successful races I'd had with seemingly little specific preparation to go that fast, and I elected to train according to my instinct for years. It was a good choice, but training is not that simple, and I suffered numerous setbacks with my training philosophies, mostly from overtraining. Whatever you do, however you train, more is not necessarily better. There are tons of ways to dig a hole for your body to fall into.

I'd lost enough confidence to turn my back on one of the cores of my training philosophy and emphasize fast training—weekly track sessions and bike intervals while backing off drastically in total training hours and long workouts. Luckily I held on to the other major aspect of my training philosophy, the Key Workouts strategy, and was able to train adequately for a while with the new monkey wrench of speed thrown in. The Key Workouts strategy is a concept introduced to me by my former coach Mark Sisson, and discussed in detail in his book, "Training for Biathlons" (he uses the term "Breakthrough workouts" and I say, interchangeably, "Key workouts").

A key workout is defined as one that is challenging enough to improve your fitness, whether it be long, fast, whatever—your body reaches a higher level of fitness when the workout is successfully completed. The strategy entails making these workouts your highest training priority and basing the entire schedule around them. I devised two simple Key Workout Strategy rules: 1) be rested for, and 2) recover from, all key workouts.

To be able to follow the rules, all other workouts in the training program are "fill in the blanks." That is, you do whatever you can—reduce, skip, or otherwise alter the workouts—to ensure the key workout rules are followed. If they are not, the key workouts are not "key." If you are not rested for a challenging workout or allow time to recover from one, the workout will not make you better. You will either train in mediocrity or break down.

Following this strategy as opposed to following a rigid daily schedule or focusing on mileage, can often result in a loosely defined, inconsistent training schedule. Who knows how much rest I'll need this week to be ready for that key long bike ride? How many days will it take to recover? Will I be rested on the day I have scheduled for the workout, or will I have to put it off and bail on my friends I agreed to meet since I'm not rested for it. Perhaps following this strategy will make you less consistent and predictable—a flaky trainer. Some athletes lose focus, but I believe the benefits of truly and honestly following the strategy are tremendous. Key workouts, when carried out properly, bring the body to a higher fitness level—the only way to race faster. The approach may seem haphazard, but I think blindly following a strict schedule, in light of all the variables in life, is more haphazard!

With this strategy, progress can be carefully monitored if the same key workout is performed and timed repeatedly, particularly considering that the workout can only take place when the body is rested for it. The graphic feedback on the progression of fitness by improving times in the same workout is even more confidence building than filling up a training log with impressive high mileage numbers, or being able to say, "I stuck exactly to my plan this week."

In the past, most of my key workouts were of the long variety. I always thought, if I can ride my bike seven hours in the mountains and feel strong, this will surely improve my 40K time. It has worked for me for years. The best cyclists in the world are the European pros who ride all day. Mike Pigg, triathlon's finest cyclist, also spends many long hours in the saddle to develop the tremendous strength he displays in short races.

In early 1994, my tune changed to, "Well, three hours is still a pretty long ride for 40K training. I'll cut my long ride back to that and focus on race pace workouts, so I won't get so tired and be able to handle the intensity of the race better, and the same goes for my run training." For longtime lightweight Brad Kearns to complete these fast key workouts regularly, long training was cut back accordingly, and rest and easy days kept popping up, so I could follow the new rules.

I started another season with the traditional warm weather double of St. Croix, Virgin Islands and St. Anthony's, Tampa Bay with decent results of seventh and fourth, respectively. Unfortunately, decent wasn't going to cut it. Furthermore, I was starting to feel the effects of my unbalanced training. There are no two ways about it; if you are unable or unwilling to spend a significant amount of time out on the road, and in the water, doing the work—building and maintaining the aerobic system, heart, lungs, muscles, and joints—intense training and racing will result in breakdown and less than world-beating performances. All other facts, rules, and strategies aside, it is unlikely that I can be a competitive pro triathlete cycling 80 to 100 miles per week and running 15 to 20 (a pseudo-pseudo-pro), with my peers who are training 150 to 300 miles on the bike and 30 to 60 running. Not that I need to duplicate what they are doing, or even concern myself with mileage (since I tell everyone else not to!). The low mileage/hours comparison was simply an observation that something was flawed in my training program.

What lay in store? Another low point in my career, this one coming in June at the Mazda/Orange County Performing Arts Center triathlon. The race carried its customary prestige on the circuit—part of the worldwide Triathlon Pro Tour, extensive media coverage, and qualifying spots for the USA team for the first ever triathlon in the Goodwill Games, scheduled for July in Russia. I placed a woeful seventh in the race. My ticket out of the sport had been printed and had popped out of the dispenser like at the movie theaters. All I needed to do was pull on the perforated edge, and I was out.

As bad as the race was, my body was worse—I could sense a breakdown looming. After another lousy performance, a third in Los Cabos, Mexico, my body shut down for summer vacation. All the intensity and not maintaining a strong aerobic base threw me completely out of whack, and as the races came and went without me at the starting line, thoughts of a premature forced retirement occupied my mind. Here I was in my ninth year of professional racing, theoretically strong and wise from all the years, and I was not even able to hold together enough to start races, let alone compete to win them. It was a do or die season, and I was dead halfway through.

The positive aspect of my fall was that I realized it was time to focus my energies on another career, rather than rely on going fast as my main source of income and dabbling halfheartedly in little side ventures. The latest of these ventures was an endurance sports radio program in Sacramento, a project I embarked on in January of 1994. The idea to host a show was inspired by Bob Babbitt, the editor and publisher of *Competitor* magazine based in San Diego. He also hosted a weekly radio program called *The Competitors*, featuring interviews of many of the world's top athletes in the endurance sports. It was a great show, and

I was honored to be a guest a couple of times after race victories. Unfortunately, the signal in Northern California was very weak, almost indecipherable, coming all the way from the Mexican border. Many Sunday nights I would frantically fiddle with the radio dial trying to pick up a word here and there of Bob's interviews. I was pretty frustrated until one day the idea came to me to host a show in Sacramento, which has a thriving endurance sports community that is almost completely overlooked by the mainstream media.

I pitched the local AM all-sports station and they said, "Sure, Brad, we'd love to have an endurance sports show, just pay us $300 for the hour each week, and then you can go sell radio commercials during your program to pay for it." I figured I could interest a few of my sponsors as well as some local merchants, to support my program since it was a unique advertising vehicle to reach endurance sports enthusiasts. After a couple of months' legwork, I had secured a title sponsor in the Gatorade company (thanks Scott Zagarino) and enough advertising commitments to sign up with the station for three months of *BK's Endurance Hour*, featuring interviews with the world's top endurance athletes, in-studio guests from the local endurance sports scene and calls from listeners.

It felt like a perfect match for my racing and my avocation of public speaking, and hopefully would be the start of a new branch of my career. I stood to make a decent amount of money off each show, provided I sold all twelve minutes of commercial time that I was allotted. The show was great fun—every week I lined up prominent guests for telephone interviews and took calls from area listeners. Quite a few of the calls came from my friends, a warm show of support, but something that caused me to wonder how many people out there were actually listening besides my friends. Whenever I'd get a call from a stranger, I'd get all excited, "Thanks *a lot* for the call, Joe Blow from Sacramento!"

After three months, I discovered that the majority of my time and energy was being spent organizing, selling, and collecting payment from the advertisers. I started to get frustrated as I was still on the hook for $300 cash each week with the station, and any difficulties I had in selling every single ad would affect me in my pocketbook. I figured I had proven myself to the station after three months, and approached them with a request to modify the terms of our agreement. The station had several full-time ad salespeople, and I thought maybe it would be nicer for them to sell my show since that was their job. I proposed this and generously offered to do the show for free, my only compensation requested was a few commercial minutes of my own to sell each week, a far less daunting task than selling 12.

The station management said they were not interested. They would rather have my check each week without expending any effort, so *BK's Endurance Hour* ground to a halt without so much as an on-air farewell from the host. It would go down in my personal history with an impressive score on my list of short-lived business ventures, ahead of the Yodolo yogurt machines and the *1991 Pro Triathlete Media Guide*, but it was nevertheless history.

Soon after the radio show was history, so was your host, BK. I spent the summer months pondering the sudden and premature end of my career. Maybe I was just used up after nine hard years on the pro circuit. I wasn't sick or anything, but not being able to train or race when my future hung in the balance indicated a need to look in other directions for my livelihood.

In my now ample spare time, I came up with a way to parlay my years of dedication to the sport and my sponsors into what I'd hoped was a solid career path. When the time came to quit racing full-time, I hoped to move into a career related to the sport, such as public speaking in the health and fitness world, writing, broadcasting, or perhaps some work with a company endemic to the sport where my name and experience on the pro circuit would be valued. The nightmare alternative to not finding a way to parlay my triathlon experience into a real career would be to head back to accounting or a similar world where I'd be just another resume with no experience, and at 29 an ancient one.

I couldn't bear the thought of stepping down from whatever high and mighty place I perceived to have carved for myself in the triathlon world and entering a new world where I was a nobody. It would mean that the nine years that I had spent would indeed prove to have been a self-indulgent vacation, rather than a stepping stone to some related career that would ideally be far more fulfilling than the suit and tie world.

Over the summer I hit up one of my oldest and best sponsors, Champion Nutrition, a company based in Northern California that markets many of the leading sports nutrition products (electrolyte sports drinks, recovery powders, supplements, sports bars, etc.) in the industry. Besides sponsoring my racing career, Champion always supported my extracurricular endeavors, sponsoring the radio program with prizes to callers, and providing product samples for everyone attending my lectures and training seminars. I sincerely believe in their products and saw the powerful effect on the audiences I addressed of my testimonials in conjunction with providing product samples. I theorized from these experiences that concentrating further on these promotional efforts would be of great benefit to a company like Champion.

The President of Champion, Greg Pickett, was immediately excited and receptive to my proposal—it looked like I had lined up a real job! Many of the details needed to be worked out, but all signs pointed to go, and I was excited to have finally developed a concrete plan to broaden my horizons in a way that was harmonious with my triathlon career.

28

ON FIRE

While I was sitting around waiting for my Champion sales career to begin—which ended up taking quite a long time—I continued with some halfhearted stabs at returning to training, each time unsuccessfully. I'd take a wcck or so off and do nothing, then set foot out the door for a run, thinking that perhaps the rest had rejuvenated me, only to struggle home after a miserable half hour. I finally concluded that although it was illogical that my body was worn out at 29, it seemed like I needed an entire year or so off from heavy exercise and competing in triathlons. Hopefully the time off would allow my body to recover from whatever the hell was wrong with it, return to an adequate state of health, and someday allow me to resume a prosperous pro racing career.

About the time that I had completely given up, I paid a visit to Mike Greenberg, a doctor in Los Angeles that I had seen occasionally over the years. He is a licensed chiropractor, but much of his practice is devoted to alternative healing methods such as applied kinesiology, acupuncture, and neuro-emotional techniques to address the influences that our emotional hang-ups and behavior patterns have on physical maladies. Many of his techniques are "out there" and not well accepted by traditional Western medicine, but his healing record is excellent. His patients include some of the top track and field athletes in the world like 1992 Olympic Gold Medalists Kevin Young (400 m hurdles) and Quincy Watts (400 m) and sprinters John Regis and Jon Drummond.

It had been quite a while since my last visit, which was unusual since normally when I run into physical problems I panic and seek help wherever I can. When my difficulties began in June, instead of exploring every avenue for help, I just resigned myself to the fact that my body had mysteriously worn out. I figured when Dr. Greenberg saw me, he would concur that I had totally fallen apart and indeed needed a year off. Andrew MacNaughton, who became exhausted after the 1993 season and had ceased training, visited Dr. Greenberg in June. Even after six months of rest, his prescription was for two more months of rest before attempting a return to training.

Early into my examination, Dr. Greenberg announced that I had a strong allergy to pollen which was sapping my strength. He treated me two days in a row, with a combination of acupuncture and a new Chinese electronic stimulation machine, announcing after the second day that I had "passed" his treatments and that my body would now to able to successfully process the pollen. His instructions were to not train for three days while my body absorbed the treatment, after which time I would feel better and be able to resume light training, with an emphasis on swimming to facilitate easier breathing.

Dr. Greenberg had always helped me with his unique treatments, but I was a bit incredulous with his prognosis. Here's a guy saying take three days off and I'm thinking, "don't worry buddy, I haven't trained in two months!" A couple of days later upon awakening my sinuses were clear. My voice, which had prompted everyone to ask me if I had a cold for the past two months, had returned to its normal tone. The third day after the treatment I tentatively headed to the pool for a swim workout, which felt surprisingly good. So did my run the following day. Then I had a decent two hour bike ride that weekend. It felt like my muscles and body were out of shape, yet my energy and health had returned. I called the doctor with the good news and asked him what the heck he had done to me!

Whatever it was, something was very different, and I was back resuming some moderate training. I was just enjoying feeling healthy and energetic again and was hesitant to even entertain thoughts of returning to the race course in the late season. I was training cautiously, always at a very comfortable pace, and soon I could sense that my fitness was returning. I got a little excited about this sudden turn of events and decided to "push it" (one of my hobbies—messing myself up by doing a workout that is way over my head at that given time just to see what happens) to check out what kind of fitness I had in me after my ordeal. I coerced my neighbor Jim Northey to join me on a one-way ride over the Sierra to Lake Tahoe, a brutal six-hour effort from Auburn with over 8,000 feet of climbing. To my surprise, coming right after two months off and in a year where my longest previous ride was just three hours, I completed the route with ease and felt fantastic. From that point on, in my mind, I was back, and not only back, but I was in that coveted state of physical and mental euphoria, only available through outstanding training and racing—I was "on fire."

The term had almost a literal meaning as my body felt like it belonged to someone else. I'd wake up early (for me) every day, feeling strong and refreshed. Instead of needing a daily afternoon nap as had been my custom the past few years, I maintained a heightened state of mental clarity and began writing this book. No more extreme physical fatigue. The contrast from my previous two and half years was so drastic, I had forgotten what it felt like to feel energized and recover normally from training.

In addition to beating the debilitating effects of the allergies, my return to training was very cautious and progressive—except for pushing it a few times—no detours on my return to competitive fitness. I was so disgusted with the failure of my early 1994 training program, and my body, that I junked all intense training upon my return to the roads. I felt like I needed to regain my strength and aerobic base, so I kept the pace comfortable for every workout, focusing on long rides and runs for my key workouts.

This change in philosophy and strategy that I happened upon in my return to training was supported by a discussion with Mike Pigg, who visited me soon after I had return to training. He had similarly altered some of his longtime training and dietary practices at the urging of his advisor, Dr. Phil Maffetone. Dr. Maffetone is an authority in the endurance sports world, and his methods are endorsed by Mark Allen, Pigg, and other top athletes. He preaches the importance of aerobic training and balanced dietary practices to maintain optimum health. The changes I made had a drastic effect on my energy, performance, and well-being. As with any training theory or program, there is no right or wrong, only what works for the individual. Dr. Maffetone's message is one of the few that emphasizes health as the way to peak performance, which made it logical and attractive to me. Many of us pursue fitness at the expense of health, often at the urging of coaches and other experts who conveniently assume perfect health is present when delivering their training theories.

Fortunately, I had a colleague of Dr. Maffetone's available to me in Sacramento, Dr. Richard Belli. Dr. Belli is an applied kinesiologist, and my regular visits to him involved a series of muscle, nerve, and reflex testing to determine functional problems in the body. Dr. Belli's treatments kept me "tuned up" during my comeback.

The first Tahoe ride was so inspiring and successful that I planned another for the following weekend in late August. I joined my friend and amateur triathlete Doug Mull for the proposed route from my home in Auburn to his cabin in Kings Beach on Tahoe's North shore, a more difficult route than the previous week's ride. Doug had never been over 80 miles in his life while this trip would be 100, almost all uphill. We left before sunrise and before we knew it, seven hours had passed and we were at the cabin. We had a comfortable day except for both suffering pretty badly on the final grueling climb over Brockway summit before descending to Lake Tahoe, but the ride was in the bank! Doug had achieved a major breakthrough mentally and physically, enough to begin entertaining thoughts of doing an Ironman. The thrill I received sharing in Doug's breakthrough, along with my personal satisfaction of continuing my comeback with the flames on high, served to boost my spirits through the roof.

We were both so euphoric that we planned to ride to Tahoe again the following weekend, choosing a far more difficult, indirect route to Tahoe's South shore, a 130-mile jaunt with over 13,000 feet of climbing. Completing it would rank up there with the most challenging rides of my life, and would dwarf anything Doug had ever attempted. Everything went smoothly for the first 100 miles, but disaster struck as we neared the top of Carson Pass, the highest point of the ride at 8,500 feet above sea level. My front tire flatted—no big deal, I'd just put my spare tire on. Whoops! The spare I was carrying was the wrong size as I had switched to a Cannondale bicycle in 1994 that had smaller 26 inch wheels, but was mistakenly still carrying a 27-inch spare tire. We were stuck in the middle of the Sierra, still 30 very remote mountainous miles from Tahoe, the nearest civilization. Not that I would be able to replace the tire there—I had called bike shops all over the Sacramento area earlier in the year looking for a 26-inch tire, but none carried any.

We were at Caples Lake, which had a seasonal resort consisting of a general store for campers, along with a bike and boat rental shop. We pedaled the 100 yards back down the road to see if the store had any tools that I could use to try to repair my flat—quite a long shot. Of course the store had nothing, and while we pondered our fate in the parking lot, a gentleman named Joe Marzocco came out of the bike rental shop and struck up a conversation. "Flat tire?" "Yeah, and I got the wrong size spare. What a bummer." "Are those 26-inch wheels?" "Yeah." "Hold on a sec." He disappeared into his shop and soon emerged with a brand new 26-inch sew-up tire, the exact same kind I had flatted! Imagine, here is this rare artifact I couldn't even locate in the greater Sacramento area, population two million, and I get one at Caples Lake high in the Sierra Nevada, year round population zero, 100 yards from where I flat. Another unsolved mystery. I guess we were meant to complete the ride, and after nine hours we did just that, arriving at Andrew's South Tahoe pad exhausted, bikes covered with fresh tar from road paving, but totally psyched from our accomplishment.

Amazingly, I felt great the following day, no soreness or residual fatigue, and two days later was up to the challenge of repeating our epic Tahoe trail run, the one that brought me out of my physical and mental funk after the World Championships exactly one year earlier. With our old swim coach Bud, the pace was aggressive the entire way, but I felt better than the previous year, even as we inadvertently tacked on an extra half hour to the loop when we got lost. That afternoon for a few fleeting moments I envisioned jumping into the Hawaii Ironman scheduled for two months later. The combination of the nine hour ride, two hour run weekend had never been topped in my training annals, and with my renewed health and energy level, it was the first time I was even able to conceive of preparing for and completing a long race successfully. It was enough trouble over the previous two years to prepare for Olympic distance races.

The thought quickly faded by the next morning; even though my training successes were over extreme distances, I knew that meant top form for a short race. Don't ask me why, and don't ask the scientists either—they'd say I was crazy. All I know is that throughout my career, if I was putting in long rides consistently and feeling strong, it translated into fast 40K bike splits in the races. The same was true for running—whenever I was able to put in a decent amount of training miles and long runs, my 10K times were fast.

I put the theory to the test when I returned to racing in late September. I chose the ITU World Cup duathlon (the new name for biathlon) in Dallas, TX. It was my first duathlon in three years and consisted of a 5K run-30K bike-5K run. The pace would be fast and furious, particularly on the first run when everyone is fresh, a situation that never exists in triathlon.

I was always weak on the first run when I raced the duathlon circuit—I just never trained to run that fast flat out, preferring to develop the strength to run well off the bike. With that history, and the fact that I had done no specific preparation for a 5K race, I was shocked to find myself with the leaders, including some of the best runners in the sport, after the first 5K in Dallas. Something was working! My training since I had returned had been more consistent than ever, perhaps since I hadn't pushed myself with intense workouts. Seemingly, the drawback to this would be that I couldn't handle intense racing without specific preparation, but I was discovering otherwise in a race even more intense than I usually competed in.

I ended up second, feeling great about my return to competition, and looking forward to the national sprint championships the following weekend in Key West, Florida. Unfortunately, I and the dozen or so other pros who traveled to Key West were greeted there by Tropical Storm #10, a deluge that buried much of the city streets under a couple of feet of water. The race was officially canceled at 4:30 AM Saturday morning. Upon receiving word, I high-tailed it out of there, drove three hours in the early morning darkness and pouring rain to Miami, and jumped on a plane to San Francisco. I had plans to salvage the weekend, for another pro race was scheduled in Santa Cruz for Sunday.

By Saturday afternoon, Pacific time, I was resting comfortably in my hotel room in Santa Cruz. I had traveled some 6,000 miles and 24 hours to get to my local Northern California race. I was less fresh than if I had just driven the 3 1/2 hours from my home to the race, but I was able to win the following day, a great positive spin to what would have been a costly and disappointing weekend.

There was still plenty of season left, including the biggest race of the year, the World Championships in Wellington, New Zealand in late November. I faced some of the favorites at the World Cup series event in Ixtapa, Mexico on October 30th, and placed fifth. I felt fantastic the entire race, catching many athletes on the run with a sub-33 minute 10K effort in the tropical heat. My swim hurt me severely as I lost the lead pack halfway, and with the new drafting legal rules on the bike, I could never make up the initial deficit and challenge for the win. I came home from the race with renewed confidence that I could run and ride with the world's best, but also knowing that the swim, my longtime weakness, would make or break me in top flight competition.

In addition to my renewed health and successful training of my comeback, I noticed something different about my attitude and state of mind before and during races. My whole life I had taken athletic competition so seriously, and cared so deeply about the results, that it naturally produced tremendous tension and anxiety before races. I was able to overcome the debilitating nervousness and dread I experienced throughout high school running, but racing triathlons was still stressful and would put me slightly on edge every time I raced.

Whatever the race, I always placed great importance on it. A big race naturally produced all those feelings, but even for the most insignificant race I could manufacture some reason to feel pressure. Maybe it was the first race of the year, or I had a cold the week before, or I was favored to win against weak competition and anything less would be a disaster—always some element of uncertainty to make the race nerve-racking.

My return to racing in September of 1994 was crucial as my future career hung in the balance. Could I really come back, or would I blow up again like I had in June? Yet when I toed the starting line in Dallas, Santa Cruz, Mexico, etc., I felt a greater sense of calm than I ever had in my career, like everything was going to be OK no matter how I finished. Some of the calmness came from the increased confidence that my body would not betray me with an empty tank on race day. My training was so much more solid and consistent that I finally felt like I was prepared and fit enough to compete, rather than needing to conjure up my secret weapon, the extra adrenaline surge I could summon for a race that would carry me to a performance greater than I thought capable of. The concept of taking my body to that place is never attractive—no wonder I dreaded stepping on the track every time in high school—it was like stepping into a torture chamber!

Knowing that my training was working and that I was looking after my body so I'd always have extra juice saved for race day made it much easier to get out of bed on race morning. I felt a little funny losing the hurried, jittery edge that was such a part of my morning ritual—I always thought it was a necessary evil of racing well. I soon realized that it was even more powerful to be in control of my emotions and nerves before a race and to feel confident that my body would respond.

The relaxed state of mind that I first felt in Dallas was facilitated by another visit to Dr. Greenberg prior to that race. With my physical difficulties successfully cured, his treatment focused on preparing me mentally to return to competition. After a treatment much briefer and less involved than usual, he announced, "OK, you're done today. I know it doesn't seem like I did much, but I just released all of the tension from your nervous system. By tomorrow you will notice a significant change in how you feel—it's hard to explain, but you will feel calmer and more relaxed."

Again, just as after my allergy treatments, all I could say was, "Whatever... thanks a lot." I flew to Dallas after the treatment, got settled into my hotel late at night, and slept like a rock for 12 hours. The next afternoon after taking care of race registration and taking a preview bike ride over the course, I took a two-hour nap. When I woke up, instead of popping out of bed right away, I laid there a while with my eyes wide open, totally alert. My body, however, felt totally lifeless, so relaxed and completely devoid of tension that I couldn't move a muscle. Each leg and arm felt like they weighed 1,000 pounds, and as I lay flat on my back looking down at them on the bed, it seemed like they weren't even my own. I thought, "What the hell did the doc do to me this time? No tension… how on earth am I going to race, or get out of bed, without a little tension flowing through the body?" It actually felt great to be so tranquil of body, yet slightly unnerving with the race looming the next day and me accustomed to my familiar drifting into the pre-race, hot-wired mode.

From the moment I awoke on race morning, I was calm and deliberate with my preparations, a complete contrast to my typical pre-race frenzied behavior. Warming up, I was content to spin the pedals easily and jog slowly, gradually preparing my body for the maximum effort of the race. Normally, before races I would feel the urge to do a bunch of sprints in my warm-ups in each sport, attempting to get pumped up for the race as well as to reassure or convince myself that my energy was there.

There's nothing wrong with doing a few short warm-up sprints, except that my reason for doing them was partly from insecurity, not knowing if I was ready to race full throttle or not. Then I'd overanalyze exactly how each little sprint felt—any sign of burning legs or sluggishness (which was almost always present, considering the body's natural unwillingness to go full tilt in the early hours of a race morning) would increase my tension.

In Dallas, I had a calmness about me that indicated unconditional confidence in my abilities. I had absolutely no idea how I would do—having not raced in three months and not raced a duathlon in three years—but I knew I would be able to perform to my current potential when the gun went off. Another factor in my calmer state was that I had come to terms with the fact that my career needed to broaden from relying solely on races for income. Just knowing that it was OK and beneficial to branch out and that I had a feasible path to take—such as working for a sponsor—eased my mind tremendously.

I knew that someday soon my career situation would enable me to not have to struggle through poor training and drag myself to races I shouldn't, simply because it was my sole livelihood. I could focus on other ways to become a productive human being—taking tremendous pressure off me and conceivably prosper more—and extend my career further since I would race for the right reasons instead of money being a priority and constant stress.

29

ONE MORE WAVE

When I surf, which is rarely and not very proficiently, a strange phenomenon occurs as I near the end of my session. Usually this comes after an hour or two of frustration, having experienced more wipe-outs and missed opportunities than epic rides. As I grow tired, I promise myself that I will catch one more wave and then call it a day. It would be absolutely unheard of to just paddle in and quit without catching a wave. Then what inevitably happens is that I catch a last wave and enjoy it so much I can't bear to quit. I just paddle back out and say, "that was so great. I'll catch one *more* wave, then I'll quit."

My triathlon career is similar. When I was facing the apparent involuntary end in the summer of 1994, I was trying to accept my fate as I had no other option. But I knew deep down that I would be disturbed that my time had come prematurely and that I had more to accomplish, like there was another wave to catch.

When I am finally faced with that choice, I wonder what I will do. If I reach a climactic point in my career—catch a great wave—I won't quit. Why quit at a peak, particularly with a strong financial incentive to continue?

Where does that leave me? I can imagine quitting if I was forced to, of course, such as if I was not generating sufficient income. And if the day comes that I feel like I had a great race, with great preparation, and still got smoked by a dozen other guys, I imagine I will be able to walk away knowing I am no longer good enough to compete at the top level of the sport and be comfortable with that realization.

My 1994 season culminated with the participation in the ITU World Championships in Wellington, New Zealand on November 27th. After missing the USA team qualifying race in Cleveland back in August, I was granted a late invitation to the race as an unattached individual entrant from the USA. I was quite happy to be able to participate in light of all the hardships I had faced over the season. The event was quite a spectacle—over 1,400 athletes from around the world converged on Wellington, and thousands lined the closed streets downtown to spectate on race day.

I felt great on race morning, again calm and relaxed about the impending event. I enjoyed the fact that I was able to remain relaxed and avoid any feeling of fear or panic, even over such a big race. I had a good swim, and by the halfway mark of the bike ride, I had moved into excellent position, riding in a large group with all the top contenders, save for defending champ Spencer Smith who was alone off the front. Then we encountered the only significant hill on the course; to my shock, my legs were dead and the pack began to drop me. I had been so strong on the hills in Ixtapa one month before, and now I was getting clobbered!

The minute I lost on the hill was my deficit behind the 20 or so athletes in the main pack at the end of the bike. A good run moved me into 13th at the finish, a little over a minute out of third place. Although my finish was respectable, second American, only a minute away from the podium, and came on the heels of a disastrous summer, it was heartbreaking at the same time. Nothing is more frustrating than being a little off peak form and then paying the price dearly in a big race.

I could go home satisfied that I did my best on that day, but upon further reflection, I realized that I had sold myself short at the World Championships. Electing to fly across the world to a race in Israel one week prior to the race was a terrible mistake. At the time I made the decision based on the financial incentive, rationalizing that I could handle the extensive travel and still be ready for the World Championships. This stacks up there with many similar ill-advised decisions I have made in my career based on greed or an unrealistic assessment of my fitness.

It is difficult to consider the possibility that my decision to race in Israel was selling myself short, and perhaps stemmed from the fact that I didn't truly believe that I could win the World Championships. In going to Israel I could create an excuse for myself, if need be, and lessen the risk involved by taking home an easy paycheck.

Upon my return home from New Zealand, I took a series of intensive training courses related to personal growth and communication. The courses were valuable and gave me the power to be truly honest with myself about my life. I took a hard look at the circumstances of my career and how I created most of them. Thinking of all the times when I felt sorry for myself for being overtrained and unable to reach my fitness goals, I realized I was unable to own up to the fact that my behavior was sabotaging my career. Instead I would rationalize something like, "Well, I'm training twice as much as normal lately, but I think I'll be able to handle it this time!"

It was much easier to tell myself that I tried my best and that everyone makes mistakes, a mind set that inhibits one's progress. When we say "I'll try" it means "I'll allow myself to fail, and that's OK because I tried." Such as when we say in everyday conversation, "I'll try to call you next week," or, "I'll try to be there around noonish," we don't mean that we are absolutely going to do whatever it takes to accomplish that what we said; we are simply giving ourselves a back door to get off the hook for failing.

Realizing that I have sold myself short repeatedly over the course of my career is very painful. It is also empowering because I can accept responsibility for my success and failure. Instead of riding shotgun, thinking I'm being driven through life by circumstances and the actions of others, I could move into the driver's seat and see that I can create whatever I want in my life.

The 1994 season was a landmark year. More so than a year of consistent finishes, 1994 taught me many lessons, some of them very difficult, but all of them serving to benefit me in the future. Experimenting with drastically different training methods steered me to the conclusion that there is no textbook answer on how best to train for triathlons—that you have to figure out for yourself what works best.

Falling apart over the summer caused me to take a look at my athletic mortality and see how much I really want to continue racing. Returning to the race course with a new, relaxed attitude made me see that I can enjoy the sport much more and feel less stress. Being honest with myself about how I sell myself short made the picture much clearer for me about my athletic potential and future intentions.

The sum of all of these experiences have helped me develop a new healthier perspective on the sport where the process of enjoying training and racing is emphasized as opposed to focusing on the results and material successes.

Ideally, my head would always be in this place, thankful to have a career that I love and to be able to use my body the way that I can, without a tremendous attachment to the outcome. But it is often easy to lose sight of one's true purpose and ideals in today's fast paced, goal oriented society. At some point, I made the decision to only be happy and content if I was racing fast or feeling strong in my training. This conditional satisfaction served to sabotage my career in many ways. For example, I would frequently force good workouts to happen, or a good week or month of training. When training is forced in this manner, for whatever reason, be it impatience, insecurity, etc., there is always a price to pay in the future.

I have paid this price many times in the form of health problems, low energy and regression of fitness due to overtraining, and poor or inconsistent race results. Often when we dig these holes, the human instinct is to push harder and thus dig the hole deeper. Instead of questioning our true intentions, we use excuses, blame and denial, and find ourselves frequently repeating the same destructive behavior.

I can think of no better vehicle to learn these lessons than through sports. To be truly successful requires a tremendous commitment in every aspect of one's being. There are great demands physically—requiring body awareness, technique, and endurance. Mental focus and concentration is imperative, along with the development and implementation of a healthy attitude and perspective. External factors like pressure, stress and anxiety must be dealt with effectively so as not to divert attention away from optimum performance.

The challenges faced and lessons learned through a sport as difficult as triathlon are all extremely valuable. It has taken me many years to realize that getting my butt kicked in a race or catching a cold from excessive, ill-advised training are valuable lessons.

Each setback is an opportunity for reflection and an honest assessment of how you got there. For example, what is it about you that thinks it's OK to abuse your body in such a way that you willfully and knowingly create a severe illness or injury like a stress fracture? When success is reached and goals are achieved is also a time for reflection. It is a common phenomenon for athletes to experience a letdown after achieving a major goal, e.g. the "post-Ironman blues." What is it about your perspective on the sport that causes you to feel melancholy after achieving a long-sought goal?

When I realize and appreciate all the lessons that participation in the sport has to offer, whether I'm breaking the tape or sitting on the sidelines watching someone else do it, is when I receive the most value and fulfillment from my career.

How would I end a book about my career? It ain't over, so perhaps I could end it with hints of a sequel, like they do in the movies: *How to Improve Your Time—the endurance athlete's guide to living a healthy, balanced and athletic life-style.*

176

Trimarket
P.O. Box 60871-B
Palo Alto, CA 94306
USA

Phone: 1-415-494-1406
Fax: 1-415-494-1413

International orders please submit an international money order drawn on a US bank.

Please send me the following:

_____ each of Can You Make a Living Doing That? by Brad Kearns at $9.95

_____ each of Scott Tinley's Finding the Wheel's Hub at $9.95

_____ each of the total runner's almanac at $12.95

_____ each of the total triathlon almanac *(second edition)* at $16.95

_____ each of the total triathlon almanac *(first edition, dated)* at $16.95

In California, add 7.75% sales tax

Shipping, within USA $3.00 ($1.00 each additional)

Shipping, priority (or international) $5.00 ($2.00 each additional)

TOTAL

I understand that I may return any unused book for a full refund if not satisfied.

Name: _____

Address: _____

finding the wheel's hub
by Scott Tinley

One of triathlon's enduring legends, this Ironman Hall of Famer tells it all in this his third book. Described by running's Bill Rodgers as, quote: "Scott Tinley brings you into the intense eye of the triathlon, spelling it out clearly and with a potent sense of humor. I found this a fascinating book."

the total triathlon almanac

is the most detailed and comprehensive of all combined training logs and training handbooks. Specifically for the multisport athlete, this almanac is described by multiple Hawaii Ironman winner Mark Allen as, quote: "the best training manual and logbook on the market (and) Highly recommended."

the total fitness log

this new multifitness book has advice from top fitness authorities. Includes sections on:

- cycling
- running
- walking
- nutrition
- swimming
- cross-training
- in-line skating
- mountain biking
- working out in the gym
- training with a heart rate monitor

the total runner's almanac

is, like its sister publication above, a comprehensive logbook and training manual, but for the runner. Described by UK *Runner's World Magazine* as, quote: "the Rolls Royce of training diaries (and) if you can only afford one running book this year, make it this one – it's worth it."

Order form on reverse page